ASCEND OR DIE

RICHARD CROSBIE

5

ASCEND OR DIE

RICHARD CROSBIE

PIONEER OF BALLOON FLIGHT

To Chris
game, set and match!

Bryan Mac Mahon

BRYAN MACMAHON

The
History
Press
Ireland

For Catherine and Amy, with love.

First published 2010

The History Press Ireland
119 Lower Baggot Street
Dublin 2, Ireland
www.thehistorypress.ie

© Bryan MacMahon, 2010

The right of Bryan MacMahon to be identified as the Author
of this work has been asserted in accordance with the
Copyrights, Designs and Patents Act 1988.

British Library Cataloguing in Publication Data.
A catalogue record for this book is available from the British Library.

ISBN 978 1 84588 985 2

Typesetting and origination by The History Press
Printed in Great Britain

CONTENTS

Those who saw him hushed.

Colum McCann
Let the Great World Spin (Bloomsbury)

FOREWORD

Of all the magnificent men in their flying machines, it was surely the first balloonists who cut the greatest dash. They were aviation's pioneers, of course: the ones who took mankind's earliest, most thrilling steps into the wide blue yonder. But they also did so with a degree of spectacle that was unsurpassed by all the pilots who came afterwards.

The problem, as was quickly discovered, is that balloons are not machines in any sense. In the frenzied few years after the Montgolfiers thrilled France with their inaugural flight (an achievement they sensibly watched from the ground), many innovations were introduced in attempts to direct these crude aircraft through the skies and to bring them down again in a controlled fashion. None quite succeeded.

As a technology, ballooning was stillborn. Within a few years, all the major improvements were already in place and the process has changed little in the two centuries since. Yet the sight of a giant balloon floating majestically across the skyline still excites the imagination as no aeroplane does. We can only guess what it must have been like to witness such a thing in the 1780s.

That Ireland has been central to the history of aviation is largely a matter of geographical accident. This island has always been a useful place to land, by intention or otherwise. From Alcock and Brown to Wrong-Way Corrigan, not to mention the Iraq war, Ireland's role has usually been that of passive observer of other nations' flights.

So it is a matter of pride that one of the first and best of the balloon pioneers was an Irishman. Richard Crosbie was every bit as intrepid as his counterparts in France and elsewhere, and no less ingenious. In some respects, he was more ambitious than his rivals – making detailed plans to bridge the Irish Sea, for example, at a time when the French still had their sights fixed on a shorter crossing: the English Channel.

His brilliance as an engineer might have been given more encouragement in Paris, where ballooning was taken most seriously from the start. Still, marginalisation did not deter him. Had the potential existed to control and direct balloon flight, Crosbie would surely have achieved it. As it was, his failures had an heroic quality.

A scientist of genuine substance, Crosbie was also a first-rate showman. He had to be. His experiments were hugely expensive and the donations of a few wealthy patrons made only a small dent in the bills. So he was also obliged to sell tickets to the public, and for a time his brilliance as an aeronaut was matched only by his skills in self-promotion.

On an unforgettable day in Ranelagh, on 19 January 1785, he rose to the occasion in every sense. Dressed in a robe of oiled silk, with satin breeches, Moroccan boots and a leopard-skin turban, he was a spectacle even before he left the ground. The thousands who had paid to watch got their money's worth.

But the demands of show business also brought pressures. Like all pioneers, Crosbie had setbacks and, in his case, they were very public. When wind conditions – the whims of which still govern balloonists today – might advise discretion, the impatience of a paying audience sometimes argued otherwise. On at least one occasion, Crosbie was forced to vow that he would fly, or die trying: something that was always possible in any case.

Bryan MacMahon's fascinating book reminds us of the insane courage of those early aviators. The quality was almost comic in the case of the first men to cross the English Channel – shedding every ounce of superfluous weight, including their trousers, in a hair-raising attempt to clear the cliffs at Calais. But there was nothing comical about the risks they faced. The glory Pilatre de Rozier won with his first flight over Paris lasted only nineteen months, before he died making his own attempt to cross the channel.

Crosbie was not just an engineer. He was also a human being, and as such he may have had a darker side. MacMahon details what is known of a disturbing incident earlier in his career that led to Crosbie spending time in prison. The book also expands our knowledge of Crosbie's later life, until now a mystery.

It was widely thought, by his friend Jonah Barrington among others, that the great balloonist had died young. With a mountain of debt behind him, this impression may have suited his purposes. But in fact, Crosbie spent many years in the US, some of it under an assumed name, attempting to recreate his glory days.

In general, it seems, his attempts to reinvent himself in America were successful only to the extent of obscuring his trail. The glimpses we get of the later Crosbie suggest a poignant picture of the brilliant balloonist's gradual drift back down to earth. Through the eyes of two men who met him in Baltimore, we get a particularly sad picture of an ageing Crosbie: still working on schemes for the advancement of science, in much reduced circumstances.

Even so, MacMahon's book does justice to a man who is now rightly considered the father of Irish aviation. Together with other recent tributes – including a statue in Ranelagh Gardens, the scene of that historic breakthrough – it represents belated recognition of Crosbie's thrilling achievements.

And in an era of mass air travel, when Irish aviation has become synonymous with the low-cost, no-frills model, this book is a welcome reminder of a more romantic era, when brave men first took to the clouds and thousands watched them in wonder, holding their breaths.

Frank McNally
The Irish Times

1

CHILDHOOD AND COLLEGE YEARS

Caelum ipsum petimus stultitia:
We storm in our folly even heaven itself.

Horace: *Odes.*

The intrepid Richard Crosbie, Ireland's first airman, was honoured in 2008 with a memorial in the Dublin suburb of Ranelagh, from where he made the first manned balloon flight in Ireland. The event took place on 19 January 1785, and drew a crowd of at least 20,000, to enjoy the unique spectacle of a man rising in a balloon and soaring across Dublin Bay. It was one of the largest crowds ever seen at a public event in the city, and the spectacle married science and entertainment in a unique way. The 225th anniversary of the first manned flight in Ireland was celebrated in Ranelagh in January 2010.

Richard Crosbie was at the centre of the balloon mania which swept Dublin in 1784-86. He deserves to be more widely recognised for his ingenuity, courage and skill. In June 1783, the Montgolfier

Memorial by sculptor
Rory Breslin in
Ranelagh Gardens,
Dublin.

brothers launched the first successful hot-air balloon in Annonay, near Lyons, inspiring others to fulfill the age-old dream of human flight. In February 1784, Crosbie first announced his intention of constructing a balloon designed for human flight; in 1785-86, his experiments in flight enthralled the citizens of Dublin and Limerick, and held them spellbound.

Richard Crosbie was born in Co. Wicklow, but the family's origins were in Co. Kerry and Co. Laois. The Crosbie line was established in Kerry in the early 1600s, when John Crosbie was appointed Protestant Bishop of Ardfert. He was originally named Seán McCrossan, a member of a Gaelic family from Laois, a branch of the O'Mores. As the old Gaelic order faced collapse, Seán McCrossan had read the signs of the times and anglicised his name to John Crosbie. He was the founder of the Crosbie line in Kerry, and another branch which was established in Crosbie Park, near Baltinglass, Co. Wicklow. Richard was born *c.*1756, the second son of Sir Paul Crosbie, 4th Baronet, of Crosbie Park, and his wife, Mary Daniel of Cheshire. Sir Paul was one of a small number of Baronets of Nova Scotia, a title which had been created in 1630, and Richard's brother Edward, born *c.*1755, inherited the title on his father's death in 1773. They had at least one sister, and they were great-great-great-great-grandchildren of John of Ardfert. In the many news reports about Richard in 1785, the Crosbies were frequently described as 'one of the most ancient and respectable families of this kingdom', but few realised that their origins were Gaelic, rather than settler.

Some little information survives about Richard's childhood, mainly from a profile of his early years published in the *Hibernian Magazine* of January 1785. Richard clearly had a talent for mechanics and engineering from an early stage. His father had the same talent, but despite this, he was concerned that his son's fascination with making things would affect his learning, and so deprived him of his tools, sometimes even to the extent of breaking them. Some of the tools had been made by the boy himself. He also broke some of the objects made by Richard,

Slaney Park, formerly Crosbie Park, the house now on the site of Richard Crosbie's birthplace near Baltinglass, Co. Wicklow.

and told his teachers to ensure that he did not indulge his passion. Nevertheless, the young inventor would lock himself into his room and continue his work, in particular making time-pieces. His perseverance and passion were impressive even then.

Richard's early schooling was in the Diocesan School, Trim, Co. Meath, a medieval stone building known as Talbot's Castle, which still stands today. A little vignette survives which confirms his intrepidity even at that stage. One of Crosbie's younger fellow pupils was said to be Arthur Wellesley, who was actually a distant cousin of his, and who would later become Duke of Wellington. One day, Richard climbed to the top of the Yellow Steeple, the tower of St Mary's Abbey, across the river from Trim Castle. At the top, as part of the caper, he wrote his last will and testament, 'disposing of his gamecocks and other boyish valuables in case he should be killed in coming down'. The piece of paper fluttered to the ground, where Arthur read it. The future military hero immediately burst into tears when he saw that nothing had been left to him. The story is related in Dean Richard Butler's history of Trim Castle (1854) and repeated in Elizabeth Longford's biography of Wellington. Butler's account confuses matters by ascribing the incident to Edward Crosbie, 'afterwards Sir Edward of balloon notoriety'. It seems a shame to spoil a good story, but in fact the two Crosbie brothers were fourteen and fifteen years older than Wellesley, so if the incident took place, it is unlikely that it was while either was at school with him.

Richard entered Trinity College in 1773, aged about seventeen. His teacher up to then was named as a Mr Franklin. He could now freely indulge his passion for engineering and science, and, maybe as a reaction to the discipline he was forced to undergo in his early years, he neglected his study while enjoying college life. His college friend Jonah Barrington gave a vivid description of him as a student, using a variation on the spelling of his name:

Crosby was of immense stature, being above six feet three inches high; he had a comely-looking, fat, ruddy face, and was, beyond comparison, the most ingenious mechanic I ever knew. He had a smattering of all sciences, and there was scarcely an art or trade of which he had not had some practical knowledge. His chambers at college were like a general workshop of all kinds of artizans. He was very good-tempered, exceedingly strong, and as brave as a lion, but as dogged as a mule; nothing could change a resolution of his once made, and nothing could check or resist his perseverance to carry it into execution.

Crosbie revelled in student life, but he failed to graduate. He was still a student in 1779, when he was reported to be the leader of a violent group of students known as the Pinkindindies, who terrorised the city for many years. On one occasion he astonished his college tutors with an inspired commentary on this text from Horace, *Nil mortalibus ardui est; Caelum ipsum petimus stultitia* (Nothing is too difficult for the daring of mortals; we storm in our folly even heaven itself). When he had made his name as a balloonist, it was recalled that he had often discussed the possibility of human flight while he was in college. He continued with his inventions, and in 1781, he designed and produced a clock 'entirely new and executed with his own hand', which his friends admired for its accuracy. As he was busy preparing his balloon in 1784, he devised an ingenious yet simple instrument for determining longitude, said to be no larger than a middle-sized watch, which worked equally well in an oven and in an icehouse. This was not just a whimsy, because timekeepers were the cutting edge of science in the eighteenth century, and there were substantial rewards for anyone who could find a solution to the question of determining longitude. Devices which could withstand extremes of temperature, pressure, and climate were urgently required for navigation. The Board of Longitude in London offered prizes to inventors of reliable timepieces, and Crosbie submitted at least one piece of work to the Board in the 1780s.

This was also the age of duelling, and the practice was almost a rite of passage. 'Does he blaze?' was the question often asked about a young girl's suitor, according to Jonah Barrington, whose brother was killed in a duel. Many young men had 'smelt powder', and killing a man in a duel was said to have been a condition of joining the notorious Hellfire Club. Barrington was himself challenged to a duel by a man named Richard Daly from Galway, one of the 'fire-eaters' who had made his name as an experienced duellist. He was reputed to have taken part in sixteen duels over two years without suffering a wound. Barrington did not know Daly and had no idea what offence he might have caused him, but when challenged, he felt obliged to accept.

Barrington chose Crosbie as his second, and received his enthusiastic backing. The first problem was that neither man possessed any pistols, but Crosbie did have a collection of old locks, barrels, and stocks from different weapons in his college room. Both men stayed up late into the night, filing, drilling and assembling three serviceable pistols from those pieces. They were 'of various lengths and of the most ludicrous workmanship', but they worked; Crosbie dryly remarked that symmetry was not an important consideration in the circumstances.

The place chosen for the duel was the field of Donnybrook fair, and, after a breakfast of hot chocolate and cherry brandy, Barrington and Crosbie turned up there at 7a.m. on a cold and sleety March morning. Barrington was startled by the first sight of his antagonist, who arrived by coach. Daly was a fine-looking gentleman, dressed in 'a pea-green coat, a large tucker with a diamond brooch stuck in it, a three-cocked hat with a gold button-loop and tassels, and silk stockings, and a *couteau-de-chasse* hung gracefully dangling from his thigh'. He already had the poise and confidence of a victor, and Barrington saw him as magnificent and overbearing. He observed that Daly had a squint, which made it 'totally impossible to say what he looked at, except his nose, of which he never lost sight'. The historian J.T. Gilbert made the same point, 'Daly had an inveterate and most distressing squint [*and*] the eye told the opposite party nothing of his intentions.'

An impatient Crosbie allowed no time for formalities, and called out, 'Ground, gentlemen ground, ground, ground! Damn measurement!' Advising his friend to aim for the hip, he whispered, 'Never look at the head or the heels: hip the macaroni! The hip for ever, my boy! Hip, Hip!' Jack Patterson, who was Daly's second, approached them saying that there was a complete misunderstanding and that Daly wished to apologise and withdraw the challenge. Barrington would have been quite happy with this outcome, but Crosbie was adamant that it was not possible. He produced a little manual of duelling, read out Rule 7, which stated that no apology could be received after the parties had met, and declared that the duel must proceed, especially since Barrington was a young man involved in his first duel against an experienced opponent.

Daly was unhappy with this, but the duel proceeded. The novice Barrington was first off the mark, and fired without taking aim. He hit Daly, who staggered back, put his hand to his breast crying out, 'I'm hit, sir!', and did not fire. Crosbie slapped Barrington on the back and vigorously squeezed his hand. Daly had a wound in his chest, but the ball had not penetrated: it had struck a brooch, a piece of which was stuck in the bone. 'Crosbie stamped, cursed the damp powder or underloading, and calmly pulled out the brooch.' Daly said nothing, merely put a cambric handkerchief to the wound, bowed and left. Barrington was greatly relieved, and inquired why the challenge had been given; Patterson then read Rule 8 of the manual, which stated that if a party accepted the challenge without asking the reason, there was no obligation to divulge it afterwards.

Barrington was generally given to exaggeration, but there is no reason to disbelieve his account of the incident. He called Crosbie 'a curious character' and mentioned that he became known as 'Balloon Crosbie' after his later exploits. He lamented that:

> ... the poor fellow, however, died far too early in life for the arts and sciences, and for friendship, which he was eminently capable of exciting. I never saw two persons in face and figure more alike than Crosby and my friend Daniel O'Connell; but Crosby was the taller by two inches, and it was not so easy to discover that he was an Irishman.

Barrington later revised his statement about his friend's early death, when he discovered that Crosbie lived far longer than his friends believed.

In December 1780, his Trinity days behind him, Crosbie married Charlotte Armstrong, daughter of Archibald, whose family seat was in Co. Offaly. At this time, he was induced to accept command of a company in a provincial regiment. This was perhaps his first attempt to establish himself in a profession and secure a means of supporting his family. He soon came to regret the decision, which resulted in considerable financial loss to him. The circumstances are only hinted at, but seem to have been caused by political machinations. Crosbie returned to Dublin, as the *Hibernian Magazine* expressed it, 'with the loss of his company and, still worse, a considerable part of his private fortune'. Financial difficulties would remain a constant feature of Crosbie's life from then on.

2

PEG PLUNKET'S REVENGE

A barbarity and savageness, at which a gang of drunken coal-porters would have blushed.

Peg Plunket, aka Mrs Margaret Leeson.

Jonah Barrington's memoirs give a vivid picture of Trinity College life at the time when he and Richard Crosbie were students there. The theatres of Dublin were very popular society venues and the wild young collegians would sometimes raid them, with these consequences:

All the ladies, well-dressed men and peaceable people generally decamped forthwith, and the young gentlemen generally proceeded to beat or turn out the residue of the audience, and to break everything that came within their reach. These exploits were by no means uncommon; and the number and rank of the young culprits were so great that, coupled with the impossibil- ity of selecting the guilty, the college would have been nearly depopulated, and many of the great families in Ireland enraged beyond measure, had the students been expelled, or even rusticated.

I had the honour of being frequently present and (as far as in melee) giving a helping hand to our encounters both in the playhouses and streets. We were in the habit of going about the latter on dark nights in coaches, and by flinging out halfpence, breaking the windows of all the houses we rapidly drove by, to the astonishment and terror of the proprietors. At other times we used to convey gunpowder squibs into all the lamps in several streets at once, and by longer or shorter fuses contrive to have them all burst about the same time, breaking every lamp to shivers, and leaving whole streets in utter darkness. Occasionally we threw large crackers into the china and glass shops, and delighted to see the terrified shopkeepers trampling on their own porcelain and cut glass for fear of an explosion.

By way of a treat, we used sometimes to pay the watchmen to lend us their cloaks and rattles; by virtue whereof we broke into the low prohibited gambling-houses, knocked out the lights, drove the gamblers downstairs, and then gave all their stakes to the watchmen ...

The young gentlemen of the university then were in a state of great insubordination – not as to their learning, but their wild habits; indeed, the singular feats of some of them would be scarcely credible now, and they were so linked together that an offence to one was an offence to all. There were several noblemen's sons with their gold-laced, and elder sons of baronets with their silver-laced gowns, who used to accompany us with their gowns turned inside out; yet our freaks arose merely from the fire and natural vivacity of uncontrolled youth: no calm, deliberate vices – no low meannesses – were ever committed.

That class of young men now termed dandies we then called macaronies, and we made it a standing rule to thrash them whenever we got a fair opportunity. Such also as had been long tied to their 'mother's apron-strings' we made no small sport with when we got them clear inside the college: we called them milk-sops, and if they declined drinking as much wine as ordered, we always dosed them, as in duty bound, with tumblers of salt and water, till they came to their feeding, as we called it. Thus generally commenced a young man of fashion's novitiate above 50 years ago.

Barrington says that as they grew older, the students left these wild ways behind and developed into upright citizens. The careers of Crosbie and Barrington provide proof of this. Dublin was indeed a place of great violence in the late eighteenth century, and college students certainly made their contribution to this lawlessness. The 'gorgeous mask' of fashionable and genteel Dublin society covered a squalid and dangerous reality. Violent deaths were a daily occurrence. 'Murder in this city has become so common that it has lost all its horrors: every day teems with new instances of the most horrid barbarity,' declared one journal in 1789. Footpads and robbers prowled the streets. The frequent running battles between the rival groups of Ormond boys and Liberty boys were a feature of earlier years, but less-organised riotous groups still fought on the streets in the 1780s. The Ormonds were mainly butchers from the quays area and the Liberty boys were weavers from around Thomas Street. The quays and the bridges had often been the scene of battles which raged for days, confining the rest of the citizens to their houses for safety. One of the punishments inflicted by the butchers was 'houghing' or cutting the tendons of an opponent so that he was lamed for life. In one gruesome incident, the Liberty boys dragged their defeated opponents to their workplaces and left them hanging by the jaws from their own meat-hooks. In what seemed like a repeat of this horror, Trinity students were once found hanging from meat-hooks, but fortunately it transpired from closer inspection that they were hanging by their belts.

Groups of collegians often raided gambling houses and stole the stakes. Some had gowns which carried distinguishing marks, but they would turn these inside out to avoid being recognised. The sleeves of the gowns proved useful for carrying the heavy keys of their rooms, which were then used a weapons to swing at victims, 'devilish good weapons on a dark night in a street wrangle or a gutter fray'. Dubliners were terrorised by a gang of gentleman-ruffians called Pinkindindies, also known as Sweaters from their practice of raiding well-to-do houses for arms and money – 'sweating'. They were typically young bucks from prominent families, who might individually seem perfectly

The College Buck. *Hibernian Magazine*, 1774. (Courtesy of National Library of Ireland.)

respectable, handsome and dashing, but who collectively were greatly feared. As gentlemen, they were entitled to carry weapons, and all were skilled swordsmen. Many of them were students of Trinity College, and there is one detailed account claiming that Richard Crosbie was a leader of the Pinkindindies. There were other lawless groups among the privileged students at that time, with names like Cherokees, Mohawks, Hawkabites and Chalkers, and they had often joined in the frequent rioting on the side of the Liberty boys. Some notorious individuals were Buck Whaley, Buck Sheehy and Buck English. Members of another group, the notorious Hellfire Club, were reported to deride the rites of religion and to set fire to any house they met in, in mockery of the flames of hell. The famous landmark ruin on Montpelier hill in Dublin was one of their reputed haunts.

The Pinkindindies' name comes from their practice of 'pinking' or stabbing people with the tips of their swords, enough to injure but not to kill. They did this by cutting off the end of their scabbards and exposing the tip of the sword, which could easily be used to jab at a person's legs to injure and intimidate them. If they were losing money in the gaming houses they would emerge and rob the first person they met. Working as a group, two would keep a look-out, while two others would jostle and jab at the victim, who usually gave up his money and watch very quickly, and made his escape; if further force were required, two more of the gang would get involved. The Pinkindindies also abducted young women on occasion, and a particularly vicious practice of theirs was to attack women in brothels and rob them of their takings; they would often have an accomplice inside the brothel among the women. They seemed to be above prosecution, although occasionally a victim might challenge them by bringing a case to court. 'They were permitted to assail people in the street, to levy contributions, to take a lady from her protector; and *many* females were destroyed by that lawless banditti', according to J.D. Herbert's account.

In July 1784, a notorious incident took place when some bucks were returning from a dinner with the Attorney General. One was a noble-

Peg Plunket. Engraving by J. Watson from painting by W. Hoare. (Courtesy of National Library of Ireland.)

man, another a colonel, and several were aides to the Lord Lieutenant. They attacked a public house owned by a man named Flattery with a view to 'sweating' him, or robbing his weapons. They abused his wife, but backed off when Flattery produced a gun, and were eventually driven away. As they left the scene, they met some soldiers and they used their military authority to order the soldiers back to Flattery's house to continue the attack. The house would have been destroyed but for the arrival of a party of Volunteers who restored order. The matter became a scandal when the Viceroy intervened to protect the men, whose identities were widely known. One of the reasons why lawless thugs continued to operate so freely was that there was no proper police force in Dublin, only an ineffective locally organised watch, usually of older men. The Pinkindindies chose their victims carefully, never attacking gentlemen like themselves, but instead ordinary citizens, who were not allowed to carry arms and were therefore easier to overcome. 'So, gentlemen never felt the pointed evil, as it never pointed at them', wrote Herbert, who called the Pinkindindies, 'an organized body of dissolute characters'.

Mrs Margaret Leeson, who was also known as Peg Plunket, was a well-known courtesan in Dublin. She was born Margaret Plunket in Killough, Co. Westmeath, daughter of a physician. Many of the country's most prominent men visited her opulent up-market brothel, originally in Drogheda Street, today's O'Connell Street. In 1795, she published her memoirs, and the three volumes are a rich source of information on her lifestyle. The Viceroy, Charles Manners, Duke of Rutland, was a client who became a particular friend. 'Honest Charley' she called him, and there seems to have been a genuine bond of affection between them. The opening of her new premises in Pitt Street in 1784 coincided with the beginning of what she described as, 'the administration of the gay, the witty, the gallant, the convivial Rutland, whose court out-rivalled that of Comus himself'. She tells the story that the Duke first visited her after an evening at the Vice-regal lodge, from where he rushed away on horseback. His aides and a troop of horse followed after, and from one o'clock in the morning till five o'clock in the afternoon, his entourage waited outside the brothel for him, thereby announcing to all and sundry where the Viceroy was being entertained. Peg boasted that hordes of people 'flocked to behold the state the exalted Peg was worshipped in by the Vice-king of the realm'.

Plunket had an exclusive clientele, including the governor of the Bank of Ireland, David La Touche, and she grandiosely described her opulent brothel as a 'Citherean temple' and her girls as *filles de joys*'. Image was all-important for her business, and Peg Plunket lived flamboyantly and fashionably; Mary Lyons describes her as 'a wealthy and beautiful *demi-mondaine*,' but above all, a shrewd business woman. She mimicked royalty, with a retinue of young women accompanying her on social occasions, such as Crosbie's balloon launch at Ranelagh in 1785. She once went to a masquerade in Rotunda gardens, outrageously assuming the guise of Diana, goddess of chastity, while her lady companions were dressed as Venus and the Graces. The theatre at Smock Alley was another popular haunt of Dublin society, and Peg frequented it accompanied by a bevy of her impures, as she called her girls, some of whom had been brought from London. The theatre was an unruly place at the best of times, with audience members often trespassing on the stage among the actors, and interrupting performances whenever they wished. At the time when she was visited regularly by the Viceroy, Charles Manners, the young bucks would call out to her, 'Who did you lie with last night, Peg?' and she would reply in mock reproof, 'Manners, you blackguards! Manners!' Great hilarity ensued, apparently even when the Duke and Duchess themselves were present. Plunket says that the Duchess was tolerant of her husband's dalliances.

The Pinkindindies met their match in the redoubtable Peg Plunket. In her memoirs, she wrote about an attack on her premises in Drogheda Street, led by none other than Richard Crosbie, whom she terms 'Mr Balloon'. The attack took place in November 1779, when Crosbie was about twenty-three. The gang was searching for John 'Buck' Lawless, Peg's companion of the time. Her fury at the way she was treated is palpable:

At that time Dublin was infested with a set of beings, who, however they might be deemed gentlemen by birth, or connexions, yet, by their actions, deserved no other appellation than that of RUFFIANS. They were called Pinking-dindies, and deriving boldness from their numbers, committed irregularities abhorrent to humanity; and gave affronts when together, which singly they would not have the courage even to attempt. They ran drunk through the streets, knocking down whoever they met; attacked, beat and cut the watch; and with great valour, broke open the habitations of unfortunate girls, demolished the furniture of their rooms, and treated the unhappy sufferers with a barbarity and savageness, at which a gang of drunken coal-porters would have blushed. At the head of this infamous set was a man who, though of noble family, disgraced it then by his behaviour; and who has since made his name famous for contriving to mount nearer to Heaven than he had any reason for expecting ever to arrive.

This person took it into his head, without any provocation, to use me in the same manner that others had been treated. He came one evening to my house in Drogheda Street at the head of a numerous gang of his associates, and insisted on being admitted. On my refusal they smashed all my windows, broke the hall-door, and entered through the shattered panels. They then demolished all the furniture of the parlours; and with drawn weapons, searched the house to find Mr Lawless, whose head they swore they would cut off, and carry away in triumph on the point of their swords, though he had not given offence to either of the party. Luckily he was absent.

This shock, with the ill-treatment I received from these self-called gentlemen, at a time when my being so very big with child, would have moved compassion in the hearts of wild Indians, threw me into a fit. I lay as dead, when some of my neighbours took me out lifeless, and carried me in that state to one of their houses.

When the watchmen came on the scene, they too were attacked, and it was only the arrival of two Sheriffs, Moncrieffe and Worthington, with military support, which finally routed the gang. Three weeks later Peg Plunket was delivered of a stillborn child who had a broken leg, caused by 'these valorous Heroes'. Peg further claimed that her two-year-old daughter, who was in the house during the attack, was so frightened and traumatised that she too died as a result:

> Thus, these magnanimous warriors actually murdered two helpless infants, bruised and mal-treated their defenceless mother, destroyed the furniture of a house, terrified a whole neighbourhood, and wounded some of the watch – for FUN. How void their hearts must be of humanity and true bravery; and how destitute of sense must be their addled brains, who can act in this manner; and whilst they act thus, and usurp the respectable name of gentlemen, can have no pretence to courage!

The house received military protection for a week after the attack, and Peg restored the damage to the building. She then defiantly laid charges against seven of the attackers, and offered a reward for their apprehension. 'When Mr Balloon heard I began a prosecution, he swore he would shoot me,' wrote Peg, 'and I on my part, openly declared I would keep a case of pistols in my pocket and blow his brains out if he approached me.' The minor participants took refuge in the country, but Crosbie brazened it out in Dublin, believing that his family status would protect him. His friends visited Peg repeatedly, threatening that they would pull down the whole house around her if she persisted with her case. Peg could not be intimidated and her answer was that she would just build it up again, and make them pay for it.

Finally, at no little expense, Peg succeeded in having Crosbie arrested and lodged in Newgate prison. (This was probably the old Newgate in Cornmarket, which finally closed in the early 1780s.) He was not allowed bail unless doctors would certify that Peg herself was out of danger, and this they refused to do. Surgeon Vance was prepared to testify that the child in her womb had died as a result of the attack, and Peg announced that she was therefore going to charge Crosbie with murder – a hanging offence. It would be a fate unimaginable for a man of his social status. Her courage and determination in challenging him

THE

L I F E

OF

Mrs. MARGARET LEESON

ALIAS

PEG PLUNKET.

WRITTEN BY HERSELF:

In which are given *Anecdotes* and *Sketches* of the LIVES and
BON MOTS of some of the most CELEBRATED CHARACTERS

IN

GREAT-BRITAIN AND IRELAND,

PARTICULARLY OF ALL THE

FILLES DES JOYS

AND

MEN OF PLEASURE AND GALLANTRY,

Who usually frequented her CITHEREAN TEMPLE for these
Thirty Years past.

THREE VOLUMES COMPLETE IN ONE.
A NEW EDITION WITH CONSIDERABLE ADDITIONS.

" She was 'tis true most FRAIL, and yet so JUST,
" That NATURE when she form'd her knew not where——
" To class her."——
" A Dame of highest VIRTUE and of TRUTH,
" Or the POOR WRETCH that she has chanc'd to be."
ANONYMOUS.

D U B L I N:
PRINTED AND SOLD BY THE PRINCIPAL BOOKSELLERS
1798.

Price sewed, 5s. 5d.

Title page of Peg Plunket's memoir. (Courtesy of National Library of Ireland.)

were quite astonishing, and her conviction of success in a legal battle against a gentleman was equally remarkable, considering the law's bias in favour of the social elite.

Richard's older brother, Sir Edward, tried to have him bailed on the basis that a fever raged in the jail, and requested that, if bail were again refused, he would be at least detained in the Sheriff's house instead. He was not successful, but at length, after pleading from the Sheriff and others, Peg decided to drop the murder charge. She was not to be utterly compliant, however, and she continued with the charge of an attack on her house. The case was heard before Judge Henn, and Peg had, 'a cloud of witnesses of the riot, assault, and destruction of my property'. A guilty verdict was reached and Crosbie was jailed. When he was released in due course after paying a fine, Peg took delight in a further prosecution, 'He thought I had forgotten him, and would proceed no farther; but revenge is sweet. I carried on my suit for damages. A second trial ensued, in which he was cast; and I had him arrested for the amount, and again put him into Newgate.' Peg was eventually paid all that was owed to her by Crosbie, and that ended the affair. She was satisfied, too, that the other attackers were still obliged to stay out of Dublin, and she took no further action against them. 'Thus ended my intercourse with that gentleman,' she wrote, although she did meet him once more.

By 1785, the formidable Peg Plunket had lost any ill-will towards Crosbie. She was prominent among those who went to Ranelagh Gardens to see his balloon flight on 19 January 1785, 'I was so far from malice when all was over, that when he was about to go up in the balloon from Ranelagh Gardens, as I thought no less than that he would be drowned, I heartily forgave, and shook hands with him.' She concludes by noting, 'But, taught by this affair, I never after would have any acquaintance with Collegians, nor ever entertained one of them.'

After the attack on her Drogheda Street premises, Peg moved first to Wood Street and then to Pitt Street, now Balfe Street. She fell on hard times and found herself in a sponging-house, or private debtors' prison, in 1794, where she attempted suicide. The publication of her memoirs was an attempt to recoup some of the money owed to her by her former clients, who had dishonoured their debts. She caused great consternation among the gentry of the whole country, who were very apprehensive about the revelations she would make. One night, as she was walking home from a visit to friends in Drumcondra, she was attacked by a gang and raped. She contracted venereal disease from which she did not recover, and died in 1797.

It is notable that Plunket placed Crosbie 'at the head of this infamous set', describing him as 'their Chief,' and later in her memoirs she referred to, 'my victory over the leader of the Pinkindindies'. In an edition of her memoirs published in 1798, she gave some added detail on the incident, referring to, 'Mr C—sby, alias Squire Balloon':

> I persecuted the ruffian and his myrmidons with the utmost rigour and obtained ample satisfaction from this chief, this modern Phaeton, by not only a year's confinement in Newgate, but recovered full damages for all the losses I had sustained ...

Strange to relate, the attack on Mrs Leeson's premises does not seem to have been referred to in any other account of Crosbie's life. The only source I have found is her memoirs. Even when he was being attacked by the press in later years, even when rivals might have wished to undermine his reputation, there is no mention of the incident. It would be reasonable to assume that newspapers would have been quick to publish scandal about a young man from a respectable family, but a scan of the newspapers around November 1779 has revealed nothing. It is possible that his family was powerful enough to suppress reports, just as the Viceroy was able to hush up the incident involving the attack on Flattery. That incident appeared in the press but not in court, while Crosbie's attack may have appeared in court but not, it seems, in the press.

Or perhaps it was just not newsworthy? It is possible that Peg

Plunket greatly exaggerated the scale of the whole incident. It seems hardly credible, for example, that a two-year-old child would die of shock because of an attack. As regards the stillborn child, there may have been other medical causes involved. Peg had five children, all of them with John Lawless, and none survived infancy. There are embellishments elsewhere in her memoirs, and many historians consider them unreliable. Dr Patrick Geoghegan has written the entry on Peg Plunket in the *Dictionary of Irish Biography* (2009) and he cautions that, 'as this autobiography was written for money and a desire for revenge, it is difficult to gauge its accuracy and authenticity'. Self-promotion had always been Peg Plunket's style and the memoirs were written to settle old scores. The sensational presentation of this incident reveals her true intentions, perhaps. She does tell the story in a triumphalist way, as an instance of her motto that revenge was sweet. Who can say for certain that the events took place as she describes them, or that Crosbie intimidated her after the incident in the way that she described? Geoghegan again rings warning bells, 'The accuracy and integrity of her account must however be questioned, and there are substantial doubts over some of her claims.' The fact that by the time these memoirs were published Crosbie was no longer in Ireland, and that many people believed he was dead, allowed Peg even further latitude in telling her story. (His brother, Edward, was, however, still living in Ireland when the memoirs were published, and was in a position to refute them, but I have not read of any response from him.)

The Pinkindindies finally disbanded in 1786, when a new police bill was being introduced, but Crosbie must have had no connection with them by then. He was prominent in press reports in early 1786, as he was planning his Limerick flight, but no connection was made between him and the news about the Pinkindindies. If he had been their leader in 1779, it is surprising that he was not mentioned in reports such as this one in the *Freeman's Journal* in April 1786:

The very sound of the police bill is said to have already made some of the gangs of robbers that have long infested the city to seek fresh quarters, from a thorough persuasion that they will have a very unprofitable season next winter in the metropolis. We hear also that the Pinkindindies have agreed to dissolve their society on or before the 29th September next. If the police bill is attended in idea with such salutary consequences, how great public good must result from its operation, when carried into practice and execution!

If Peg Plunket's account is true, then Crosbie's actions in November 1779 were reprehensible. If he threatened and intimidated her after the incident, as she described, then his reputation is tarnished. However, it seems certain, at least, that Crosbie did not set out that evening with murder on his mind. The man of whom we get some glimpses through press reports seems to be an utterly different character from the one described by Peg Plunket, and there is a strong inclination to believe that she exaggerated the incident. In the 1780s, Crosbie's courage and intrepidity were admired by newspaper editors, he was hailed as a hero by the public, and he was supported by men of the highest distinction and authority in Ireland. If he had indeed spent a year in prison after the attack, it is hardly likely that the Armstrong family would have acquiesced to his marriage to Charlotte in December 1780, when he would have just been released. If he had been a callous thug, and an ex-convict, the Dukes of Leinster and Rutland and the Earl of Charlemont would hardly have supported him so readily and so loyally. Charlemont not only admired the courage and determination of his friend 'the aerial Crosbie', but felt genuine affection towards him. In 1786, he described him as, 'an excellent man ... calculated to be a most useful member of society' and as, 'a truly amiable and sensible man'. On balance, in the absence of any corroboration, it seems best to reserve judgement on the accuracy of Peg Plunket's account of events, and to trust the opinions of men such as Charlemont.

In a book published in 1847, John Walsh told the story of a distinguished young Trinity College student named McAllister, who, like the

Richard Crosbie medal of 1780.

Pinkindindies, wore his sword with the tip uncovered. After a drinking bout, he got involved in a brawl and killed a man on the street.
He escaped punishment by fleeing to America. McAllister was held in
high esteem by all who knew him and Walsh's comment on him might
apply equally well to the situation of Richard Crosbie, 'He was a young
man of a most amiable disposition. Had he lived in better days, he
might have been distinguished for gentleness and humanity; the spirit
of the times and the force of example converted him into an atrocious
murderer.' If it is true that Crosbie was leader of the Pinkindindies,
and behaved as described by Peg Plunket, in later times he must have
been deeply mortified (a word he frequently used in other contexts)
by his actions, and the consequences of the wildness and aggression
of his student days. Since Peg Plunket was gracious enough to forgive
Crosbie, perhaps history can forgive him also. As Barrington explained
their student excesses, 'Our freaks arose merely from the fire and natural vivacity of uncontrolled youth.'

There is one final glimpse of Richard Crosbie in the days before
his balloon adventures began. It dates from August 1780, when,

according to Peg Plunket's account, he was in jail, and it was special tribute paid to him and his work on behalf of an unusual theatre company in Dublin. A medal which came up for auction in England some years ago had an inscription which read:

> The Microcosm Society present this medal to Richd. Crosbie Esqr. in token of the Great Attention shown by him in the Construction of the Microcosm Theatre and for the Eminent Ability display'd by him in the execution.

The date on the reverse is 'Aug. 4th 1780'. This is a further indication of the esteem in which Crosbie was held at this time, undermining Plunket's claims. The Microcosm Theatre was a marionette or puppet theatre which flourished in Drury Street, (formerly known as Booter Lane) from 1779 to 1781, and perhaps longer. There had been a previous puppet theatre in Abbey Street, Mr. Punch's Patagonian Theatre, managed by John Ellis, whose puppets were later used in the exclusive Microcosm Theatre. Clearly, Crosbie's technical design and construction skills were much appreciated by the society. Just a few years later, he used his skills to design and construct an 'aeronautic chariot'.

❦ 3 ❦

THE FIRST AERIAL ADVENTURERS

Of what use is a new-born babe?

Benjamin Franklin

In June 1783, the Montgolfier brothers in the village of Annonay, near Lyons, launched the first hot-air balloon, prompting others into immediate experiments. The Montgolfier family owned a paper-making factory and the brothers are said to have noticed how paper floated upwards over a fire, or alternatively to have observed a shirt or chemise filling up with air and floating over a fire. They experimented on a small scale at home and eventually were confident enough to arrange a public display in the nearby village. They made a balloon of canvas lined with paper, sealed the sections of material with buttons, and on 5 June 1783, took it to the village square. They amazed the onlookers by successfully flying the balloon, which had a circumference of 110ft. It flew for around ten minutes, rising to about 6,000ft, and landed a mile and a half away. It fell as a result of hot air leaking through the button holes. Believing that they had discovered a new gas, and that it was generated within the smoke of a fire, they tried to produce as much smoke as possible, even using old leather and rotten meat, with the result that their early flights were murky and malodorous.

When word of their experiments reached Paris, members of the Academy of Sciences were taken aback at the successful experiment by mere provincial businessmen, and were spurred into action. Professor J.A. Charles had been aware of a new gas which was called 'inflammable air' or hydrogen, and knew that it was much lighter than air. Hydrogen was first identified by the English scientist Henry Cavendish and called 'phlogisticated air'. With the help of skilled craftsmen, the brothers Aîné and Cadet Robert, Charles constructed a balloon made of silk, sealed with a coating of rubber, and filled it with hydrogen. It was 12ft in diameter, 36ft in circumference, weighed 26lbs and had a capacity of 943 cubic feet. The hydrogen was generated by the action of sulphuric acid on iron filings, and was then conveyed into the envelope by a complex system of barrels and pipes. It took 498lbs of acid and 1,000lbs of iron to generate enough gas to fill the balloon.

Charles' balloon, called the *Globe*, aroused unprecedented interest, and was released from the Champ de Mars, where the Eiffel Tower now stands, on 27 August 1783. A huge crowd, including many with a scientific interest, observed the *Globe* as it rose to about 3,000ft and disappeared into the clouds. It landed forty-five minutes later near the village of Gonesse, where it caused a sensation. Villagers thought it was some kind of marauding monster, and attacked it with muskets and pitchforks. The French government felt obliged to issue this warning to the public:

It is proposed to repeat these experiments on a larger scale. Any one who shall see in the sky such a globe (which resembles 'la lune obscurcie') should be aware that, far from being an alarming phenomenon, it is only a machine, made of taffetas, or light canvas covered with paper, that cannot possibly cause any harm, and which will some day prove serviceable to the wants of society.

The next major public exhibition was the launch of a balloon by the Montgolfier brothers from the Palace of Versailles, in the presence of the King Louis XVI and Queen Marie Antoinette. The royal couple enthusiastically supported the experiments, but kept a discreet distance on account of the smoke and smells. This was on 19 September 1783, and the balloon was made of cotton with a paper lining, with the sections sewn together rather than buttoned; it was 57ft high and 41ft in diameter, with a capacity of 36,500 cubic feet and beautifully decorated in blue and gold. The king had vetoed any suggestion of a human being on board, because of the risk to life, and it was decided that the passengers should be a sheep, a duck and a cock. Most of the onlookers had no idea what might happen in the upper air and whether people could even breathe up there, so the fate of the animals would determine future plans. The flight lasted only about ten minutes and the balloon landed over two kilometres away, the wicker basket breaking open as it hit the ground. The sheep was discovered grazing contentedly, the duck quite placid too, but the rooster was somewhat worse for wear. This caused some concern, until witnesses swore that they saw the sheep sitting on the cock before the flight. The whole demonstration was regarded as a great success and generated a huge amount of public interest.

The next challenge was to attempt a manned flight. The Montgolfier brothers apparently had promised their worried father that they would not ascend in a balloon, so there was some discussion as to who would be chosen. Louis XVI suggested that two criminals should be sent, as he fully expected that they would be killed. It was quickly pointed out that, should the experiment succeed, it would not be seemly to have two criminals as great heroes. So it came about that a scientist named Pilatre de Rozier, and the Marquis d'Arlandes, an aristocrat, were the first men to fly in a balloon, on 20 November 1783. The balloon was 75ft high, 49ft in diameter and had a capacity of 79,000 cubic feet. After days of trial flights with captive balloons, the two men took off from the Bois de Boulogne in Paris and flew at low altitude for about twenty-five minutes, landing near the present Place d'Italie, only 9,000 yards from where they set off. The historical significance of the event was immense, 'The slender navel string that till now had still linked man to his mother earth was severed and for the first time in the history of the world, man rode freely and proud upon the limitless plain of air.' (L.T.C. Rolt). Nevertheless, the whole event had its comical and dangerous aspects too. The men were in a gallery at the base of the balloon, rather than in a basket; for balance, they were on opposite sides and so could not see each other. They communicated by shouting, with de Rozier constantly exhorting the Marquis to work harder at feeding the fire, while the latter was overawed by the spectacular view of the city, and anxious to descend as soon as possible. The danger of falling into the Seine was very real; sparks were flying on to the fabric, burning little holes, and they had to use sponges to douse these.

First manned flight. (Courtesy of Robert Tressell Family Papers.)

The first manned flight
in a hydrogen balloon.
Hibernian Magazine, 1784.
(Courtesy of National
Library of Ireland.)

Meanwhile, J.A. Charles was also intent on a manned flight in his
hydrogen balloon. This was achieved by Charles and Ainé Robert on 1
December 1783, from the Tuileries Gardens. There was by now a balloon
frenzy in Paris and a crowd estimated at 400,000 was present – almost
half the population of the city. The technical procedures were complex,
time-consuming and dangerous, as a massive quantity of hydrogen had to
be generated and conveyed into the envelope. The balloon was a perfect
sphere 27ft 6in in diameter, and made of stripes of red and yellow silk.
The upper half was covered in netting and there was a hoop, or *cerceau*,
at the centre of the envelope, to which the car was attached. The design
and the safety valves adopted by Charles were followed by balloonists for

many years afterwards, and the basic elements of modern gas ballooning were established in this first flight. The hoop was found to cause chafing and leakage, so it was later adapted. The car was 8ft long and 4ft wide, and was elaborately decorated. Joseph Montgolfier was present at this launch and, although there was said to be rivalry between the promoters of the different types of balloon, Charles generously acknowledged the Montgolfier brothers' pioneering role by inviting Joseph to release a trial balloon to indicate the wind currents, with the words, 'It is for you, monsieur, to show us the way to the skies.'

The spectators fell into an awed silence as the balloon rose majestically, and cheered once it was clear that the launch was a success. The balloon reached a height of 1,800ft in a few moments, much more quickly than a hot-air balloon. The flight lasted for two hours and the two men obviously relished the experience. They had brought on board instruments such as a barometer and a thermometer, ballast of sandbags and provisions which included bottles of wine. A gift of wine helped to mollify a farmer whose crops might be damaged by a balloon landing; this tradition continues on occasion today. After gliding over the city and observing all its wonderful sights from a novel perspective, they made a perfect landing near the town of Nesles, twenty-seven miles from their starting point. Charles was so pleased with the experience that he set off alone immediately for another flight of about thirty-five minutes, shooting up at an alarming speed of about 1,000ft per minute. In what was the world's first solo flight, Charles was exhilarated, and claimed to have been the first man to see the sun set twice in one day. 'I could hear myself living, so to speak,' he enthused, 'it was not mere pleasure, it was perfect bliss'. Strangely, although he showed a tremendous ability to control the balloon, he never again flew in one.

From this time, hydrogen balloons were called Charlieres, and hot-air balloons were called Montgolfieres. The Montgolfieres, with a brazier on board, and a fire which was usually fed with a mixture of straw and wool, were highly dangerous as well as labour intensive, and water had to be carried on board as a basic safety precaution. The Charliere was a more expensive balloon, requiring more technical preparation, but had the advantage of being far lighter, cleaner, and easier to manage. The level of public interest in the experiments was astonishing, as were the commercial possibilities presented. As Richard Holmes expressed it, 'With ballooning, science had found a powerful new formula: chemistry plus showmanship equals crowds plus wonder plus money.'

The first manned balloon flight from British soil was on 25 August 1784, from Edinburgh, by James Tytler, an eccentric character from a humble background. He constructed a barrel-shaped Montgolfiere balloon, with a huge furnace and an elaborate boat, but when this failed to ascend, and his impatient spectators began to express their displeasure, he dispensed with the furnace and the boat, and simply attached an ordinary crate to the balloon. It rose to only 500ft, and dropped quickly; Tytler himself modestly described it as more of a leap than a flight. Tytler was editor of the second edition of *Encyclopaedia Britannica*, but when he espoused republican principles he had to flee the country, first to Ireland and then to Salem, in America, where he became the editor of a radical journal.

The first man to fly in England was an Italian named Vincenzo (Vincent) Lunardi, who became a much-celebrated figure. He was a vain man, a dandy and a showman who richly enjoyed the acclaim and hero-worship that followed his flight from the Artillery Grounds at Moorfields in London on 15 September 1784. He was undoubtedly fearless and spirited, as well as impulsive, flamboyant and lucky. There were about 150,000 people at the launch, and being obliged to wait a long time until all was in a state of readiness, they grew restless. An affray broke out when some people said that their view was blocked by coaches of the well-to-do; then a rumour went around that a bullock was running amok in the area, and finally, a makeshift stand collapsed. Just weeks earlier, a Frenchman named de Moret had organised a flight from London, but his balloon caught fire before lift-off, and the angry and frustrated spectators then attacked him.

Aware of the dangers of a volatile crowd, Lunardi set off before the balloon was fully inflated; he had a cat, a dog and a pigeon in the basket, and he carried oars, which he believed would allow him to control

Vincent Lunardi. *Hibernian Magazine*, 1784. (Courtesy of National Library of Ireland.)

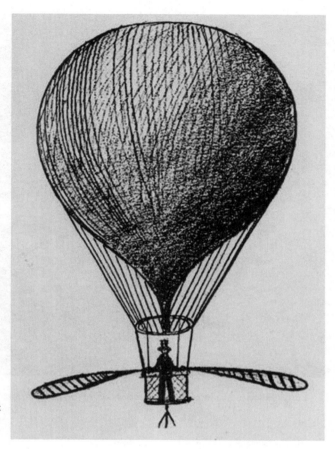

Lunardi's balloon.
(Courtesy of Robert
Tressell Family
Papers.)

the balloon in the air. As he rose, the crowd fell into an awed silence, and then followed the lead of the Prince of Wales by raising their hats. Lunardi himself wrote:

> The effect was that of a miracle on the multitude which surrounded the place, and they passed from incredulity and menace into the most extravagant expressions of approbation and joy … I had soared from the apprehension and anxieties of the Artillery Ground and felt as if I had left behind me all the cares and passions that molest mankind.

Lunardi's second balloon flight. (Courtesy of the Board of Trinity College Dublin.)

Many in the crowd were convinced that Lunardi would not be seen again. He was quite composed, however, and in control; he travelled for over two hours, eventually landing safely in a field near Ware in Hertfordshire, twenty-four miles away. A commemorative plaque still stands on the village green:

Let posterity know, And knowing, be astonished! That on the 15th day of September 1784, Vincent Lunardi of Lucca in Tuscany, the First Aerial Traveller in Britain, Mounting from the Artillery Ground in London, and Traversing the Regions of the Air, For two hours and fifteen minutes, on this Spot revisited the Earth ...

The dashing Italian became the hero of the hour, and a great favourite among the ladies. He was received at court, lauded by the press and immortalised in ballads. There were Lunardi bonnets, wigs, coats, and even garters for his multitude of female admirers. The balloon symbol adorned china, porcelain, prints, fabrics and jewel cases. The balloon theme went further than clothing: a fashion for breast enhancement was taken advantage of by two women in Paris, as reported in the *Dublin Evening Post* of May 1786:

> The present fashionable protuberances so much in vogue among the females have by the adroitness of two dressy fair ones of this capital, been turned to a profitable instead of expensive fashion ... The females in question had contrived to fill bladders with brandy which they had substituted for cork, wool, wire &c and thus equipped in the most outré prominence of the mode, they passed several times daily through the gates of Paris smuggling not inconsiderable quantities of brandy.

The guards suspected what was happening, and when one pierced, 'what nowadays is normally made of cork, a fountain of brandy played from the orifice, to the great diversion of the spectators and the no small confusion of the fair one'.

Lunardi succeeded in winning over the British public, who had previously been sceptical of French experiments with balloons. In France, the scientific and research potential of balloons was paramount, but in England the entertainment aspect was more to the fore. In many subsequent flights in England and Scotland, Lunardi gave value for money, and organised the first flight in England by a woman, Mrs Sage, in June 1785. She and her male companion enjoyed a lunch – with wine – as they glided over London, to land in Harrow. When in Edinburgh, Lunardi followed the example set by J.A. Charles, and graciously acknowledged Tytler's achievement before him. The commercial potential of ballooning was highlighted when the aeronauts' accounts of flights were acquired exclusively by some journals, and both Lunardi and Mrs Sage published accounts of their experiences.

Lunardi also had his critics however. An early historian of flight, Tiberius Cavallo, in 1785, regretted that he made no scientific investigations and merely courted fame and attention, 'The enthusiastic applause with which he was afterwards honoured, and perhaps poisoned, have exposed him to a variety of scrutinies and remarks, which were dictated generally by envy and often by misinformation, but sometimes by justice.' As early as July 1785, *The Gentleman's Magazine* described his unimpressive flight from Liverpool and commented, 'It had been fortunate for this gentleman if he could have been contented with the honour he had gained by his first exploit. He seems to have lost ground by every later attempt.'

In reality, Lunardi was highly popular for two years as he travelled around Britain. Dublin had a visit from the great aeronaut in 1786, and his declared intention was to complete a crossing of the Irish Sea, a much longer undertaking than the English Channel. This seems to have been a direct challenge to Richard Crosbie's efforts, and he met with so little support in Dublin that he returned to England without making any flight.

Lunardi was eventually obliged to leave England after the public turned on him following an unfortunate accident. As he was preparing to ascend from Newcastle-upon-Tyne in August 1786, the men holding the retaining ropes relaxed their grip and the balloon flew up with the ropes entangled around the arm of a young man who was lifted away. The rope broke and he fell to earth from a great height and was killed. The press and public now began to attack Lunardi, blaming him for causing the death, and he eventually returned to Italy. He continued to make balloon flights there and in Spain and Portugal for many years after. When he landed in one Spanish village, he was hailed as a saint descended from heaven, and was carried in procession to the church.

The first Englishman to fly was James Sadler of Oxford, in October 1784. He made several successful flights, but after a few brushes with death, he abandoned the air in 1785 and chose to turn his scientific talent to making improvements on the steam engine. Remarkably, he

James Sadler. (Courtesy of the Board of Trinity College Dublin.)

returned to ballooning twenty-four years later with his two sons, and the Sadlers played a significant role in the history of Irish ballooning in 1812 and again in 1817. One result of the balloon craze was the proliferation of small experimental balloons being released by the public. It was relatively easy to make a small Montgolfiere balloon and send it off, but the fire element presented a grave danger. Catherine the Great in Russia banned balloons altogether, and other countries introduced often ineffective by-laws to curtail the practice.

The earliest reports in Dublin of these experiments were suffused with awe and wonder. The *Hibernian Magazine* of October 1783, commenting on the first experiments with balloons, speculated on the possibility of 'flying or rather swimming through the air', and noted that 'there has ... actually been made an offer by some poor devil, reckless of life and hoping for reward, of his body for the first attempt'. It also attempted to explain the science behind the new machines, confusingly describing the balloons as filled with 'inflammable air or aether' or 'fumous particles':

> As it is in the nature of flame to ascend, so the globe by means of the fiery particles it contains, will continue to ascend or at least float and resist the attraction of the earth till the internal aether has evaporated, and then the globe, in obedience to the laws of gravitation, must necessarily fall.

The story of the two criminals also appears in the *Hibernian Magazine*. It says they were 'condemned to be broke upon the wheel' and offered instead to go up in a cage attached to a balloon, on condition that they would be pardoned if they survived. The journal noted that they were choosing an easy death in the air over a crueler one on the ground.

At the dawn of ballooning, Benjamin Franklin was in Paris and took a keen interest in the developments. He wrote regularly to Sir Joseph Banks in England, describing the balloon displays. The story goes that when Franklin was asked, 'Of what use are these new machines?', his reply was, 'Of what use is a new-born babe?' The ailing Dr Johnson was interested in ballooning but also sceptical of any benefits. 'We now know a method of mounting in the air,' he wrote, 'and I think, are not likely to know more.' The English writer Horace Walpole, was equally unenthusiastic, and voiced his deepest fears about the future, 'I hope these new machines will prove playthings for the learned and the idle, and not be converted into new engines of destruction to the human race as is so often the case with refinements or discoveries in science.' A correspondent of the *Hibernian Magazine* was one of those quick to pounce on that very prospect, predicting that balloons could be adapted to warlike purposes, and foreseeing that, 'ingenious mechanics would build men-of-war calculated to sail through seas of ether and treat the world to sights of aethereal combats'. He added provocatively that, 'the French may then surely call themselves sovereigns of the air'.

There was considerable trepidation in Britain about this French discovery and the military uses to which it might be applied. In the 1780s, the British occupation of Gibraltar was much in the news and there was speculation that it could easily be taken by an invading force from the air, and even that Britain itself could be invaded by the French. Balloons were in fact used for military purposes for the first time at the battle of Fleurus in 1794, where tactics were directed from a balloon, and the result was victory for the French over the Austrians. Much later, balloons were also used during the American Civil War, and during the siege of Paris in 1870, when sixty-six balloons left the city carrying approximately a hundred passengers and two and a half million letters. This has been described as the first air-lift in history.

By January 1785, almost 200 manned flights had taken place in France and England. Jean-Pierre Blanchard, a Frenchman who had a grand plan for crossing the English Channel, was to become one of the most successful pioneers of the air. He was among the first to identify the problem of navigation as the key issue for the future of ballooning, and he set about adding various devices to solve this. These included oars, rudders, sails and a *moulinet*. The last item was a windmill-type addition to the side of the boat. Blanchard's motto was *'Sic itur ad astra'* – Thus one reaches the stars. After one of his displays in France, he was assumed to have made an easy profit:

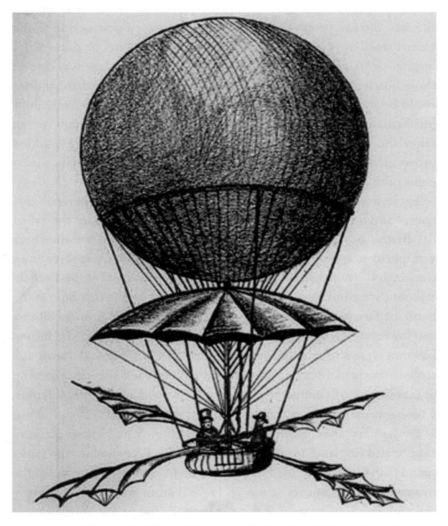

One of Blanchard's balloons. (Courtesy of Robert Tressell Family Papers.)

Au Champ-de-Mars ils'envola,
Au champ voisin il resta la,
Beaucoup d'argent il ramassa,
Messieurs – sic itur ad astra.

(From the Champ de Mars he flew/ Into the next field he fell/ Plenty of money he gained/ Sirs – sic itur ad astra.)

Blanchard moved to England in the autumn of 1784, continuing his experimental flights there. He was then fortunate in attracting the support of a wealthy American scientist, Dr John Jeffries, who collaborated with Blanchard for genuine scientific purposes. He wished to explore the effect of oars and wings in directing the balloon, wind currents and temperature changes at altitude, and methods of ascending and descending. In a trial flight across the Thames, Jeffries carried a thermometer, a barometer, a hydrometer, and an electrometer; he also took maps, compass, note-taking materials, and flasks to collect air samples.

Jeffries undertook to put up £700 to finance the cross-channel flight, in return for a place in the balloon with Blanchard. The wily aeronaut gladly accepted the money, but tried several ruses to prevent Jeffries from accompanying him, in order to retain the honour of the historic flight solely to himself. Finally, Blanchard grudgingly allowed Jeffries on board, limiting his equipment to a barometer and a compass. They set off from the cliffs of Dover at 1p.m. on 7 January 1785, dressed for the winter weather and taking the precaution of including cork jackets in case of emergency. The two men became the first to complete a sea crossing by balloon, out-stripping their main rivals, James Sadler and Pilatre de Rozier, who had plans for the same feat.

Jeffries wrote a vivid account of the exciting and dangerous two-hour journey. As they progressed, the balloon was dropping in height all the time. Item by item, they were obliged to drop their sand ballast, parcels of books, and food; still dangerously low, they cast away one wing, then the other, and then the *moulinet* was unscrewed and discarded, to be followed by ropes and anchors. Still dropping, and only 120 yards above the surface of the sea, they then removed and discarded their great-coats, followed by their trousers. They were now preparing to attach themselves to slings under the balloon and cut away the car itself. Jeffries also offered to jump into the sea, in order to ensure Blanchard's success, when, about four miles from the French coast, the balloon finally gained enough height to clear the cliffs at Calais. Their adventure was not yet over, however, as they were now driven inland at high speed and looked like they were about to make a crash landing about twelve miles from the coast. In one last effort to ensure a safe descent, they lightened their load by urinating into a leather bladder which was part of the rigging, and throwing it overboard. Although decorum prevented Jeffries from explicitly saying so, he implies that they also lightened the load by defecating. They finally came down in a forest, wearing only their underclothes and cork jackets.

This bizarre journey was truly historic, and Paris acclaimed the two heroes. Jeffries never flew again, but Blanchard went on to complete over sixty flights, including the first flights in Germany, Belgium, Poland, Holland, Switzerland and the United States. He was the most skilful of the early balloonists and he became a professional aeronaut, as did his second wife, Sophie.

What has not been fully acknowledged by historians of early flights is that Richard Crosbie was also in the race to make the first sea-crossing by balloon, from Ireland to Wales, and that he came close to accomplishing it. He first set out his plan in August 1784, and, after many delays, fixed his flight for the autumn. When that proved impossible, he announced that it would happen in December. That date also passed, and he then chose 4 January 1785 as his launch date, three days before Blanchard and Jeffries actually set off from Dover. This date too passed, and Crosbie finally got off the ground on 19 January. How much Crosbie knew of the achievements or plans of other balloonists in France and England is not clear, but his objectives were at least running parallel to theirs. Hodgson quotes Blanchard as commenting that 'the Irish have hearts but not heads for ballooning', but the date and context are not given, so it is impossible to say if he was referring to Crosbie – or if Crosbie was goaded by the remark.

It is interesting to note that the paths of these two pioneers of balloon flight may have crossed many years later, when they were both in New York in 1796-97.

❦ 4 ❧

PLANS AND DELAYS

This gentleman is a native ... (and hopes) to see every art for the good and ornament of his country brought to perfection.

Hibernian Magazine, 1784.

At the end of January 1784, the Liffey in Dublin was a sheet of ice and several people took the opportunity to dazzle passers-by with their skating prowess. Richard Crosbie might have seen the young skaters on his way to and from his house in North Cumberland Street, and strengthened his resolve to win his own measure of public acclaim by something much more daring. His exploit would lift the gaze of the populace upwards, into the unexplored region of the air. He was also spurred into action by hearing of the first Irish balloon flight organised by a Mr Riddick on 4 February from Rotunda Gardens. The *Hibernian Magazine* lamented that the balloon was small – 6ft in length and 4ft in diameter – and that it did not carry passengers '*a la mode de Paris* in an attendant triumphal car'. It went on to welcome the following announcement by 'an ingenious gentleman' which appeared in the press on 7 February 1784; it is the first recorded declaration of intent by Crosbie.

A gentleman of this city who has long endeavoured to exercise his mechanical abilities for the general service and has some reason to flatter himself with every prospect of success has opened a subscription for defraying the expense of making an Aerial Chariot ... on a plan large enough to take two men with all their necessary equipment; he has invented a mode of conducting and managing it through the air in whatever direction he chooses ...

This gentleman is a native and has been a constant inhabitant of this kingdom, he therefore hopes that as his wishes are as ardent as any person's can be to see every art for the good and ornament of his country brought to perfection, he may have an opportunity of obtaining the honour of submitting his plan to the judgement of the country. He means to ascend in it himself and show the way to manage it; any subscriber who chooses can accompany him. He does not come from another country to impose on the imagined ignorance of this by exhibiting a child's bawble to the curious multitude from an air balloon which must rather tend to prejudice the public against the utility of such a vehicle ...

Subscriptions will be received by the following gentlemen: Rev. Dr. Usher and Arthur Brown Esq., Fellows of Trinity College Dublin, Mr. Edward Hudson, Grafton St. and Richard Crosbie Esq., 28 Nth. Cumberland St.

No eighteenth-century buildings remain today on the once-fashionable street where Crosbie lived, so it is not possible to identify his house. It is notable that Crosbie's Irishness is stressed from the outset, and the references to another person exhibiting a child's bauble probably refers to Riddick, whose balloon was most likely a Montgolfiere type. Riddick was the first of a small number of rivals to Crosbie on Irish soil, against whom he regularly played up his Irish background and identity, and his motivation to bring glory and honour to his native land.

Even if Crosbie had left Trinity without a degree, it seems that he was in good standing with its leading lights, such as Provost John Hely-Hutchinson, Dr Henry Ussher (Usher was the usual spelling in newspapers) and Dr Arthur Brown. Ussher was the first Professor of Astronomy in Trinity and founder of Dunsink Observatory, and his involvement highlights contemporary hopes for the scientific potential of ballooning. Balloon developments in France were supported by the academies and scientists expected to learn much about weather and the atmosphere, while in Britain balloon flights were mainly for entertainment. Crosbie gained active support too from the Lord Lieutenant (the Duke of Rutland), Lord Charlemont, the Duke of Leinster and many other influential public figures and patrons of the arts and sciences. There was also a very brief report in a newspaper that 'a distressed family received 3s 3d anonymously via Mr Crosbie', suggesting that he was seen as a man of probity. All newspaper references to Crosbie indicate that he was a man of honour and integrity, inspired by patriotism and the spirit of scientific inquiry, and there is no hint of scandal or any reference to a disreputable past. This confirms the wisdom of treating Peg Plunket's story with scepticism.

In this first declaration, Crosbie also addressed one of the biggest problems bedeviling early balloon experiments: the lack of control when in the air and the fact that the balloon was entirely subject to wind conditions. He told the public that he had devised a mode of piloting his balloon to ensure that he could travel in whatever direction he wished, and that he would, 'show the way to manage it'. This would have marked a significant improvement on all previous models, but it remained to be demonstrated in practice. The early balloonists faced four significant problems, namely:

How to make a balloon (or envelope) which would combine lightness and solidity and would be impermeable to air;
how to find a gas which was inexpensive, always available and easy to obtain;
how to find a method of ascending and descending at will;
how to find a simple method of directing the machine.

The first problem was solved by the use of rubberised silk; the second with hydrogen gas; the third by skill, scientific calculations of weight and ballast, and mastery of intricate valve systems. The final problem was a challenge for all the early balloonists. In late 1784, Lunardi was using oars to try to direct his balloon, and Blanchard also used oars or paddles in his crossing of the Channel. Faulkner's *Dublin Journal* was the only newspaper to highlight explicitly the significance of Crosbie's claim to be able to guide his balloon, crediting him with the discovery, 'As the power of directing this machine is the grand desideratum, and appears to be the only improvement which can render it of any particular utility, we are glad for the credit of Irish ingenuity that the honour of this discovery originated with ourselves.' Crosbie had taken on the challenge identified by the anonymous writer of these lines, 'To Montgolfier the Invention's due,/ Unfinish'd as it lies,/ But his will be the glory who/ Direction's art supplies.'

While in the year 1783 aquatic experiments and diving machines had been the talk of the town, the *Hibernian Magazine* declared in early 1784 that, 'aerial chariots, air balloons, aerostatic globes, spheres, etc., etc. now are the only fashionable topics'. Crosbie impressed Dr Ussher, who invited him to his college chambers where Crosbie explained his scheme to an interested group. Ussher wrote privately to the Earl of Charlemont in early April that, 'his present scheme seems to me to afford some prospect of success; still, however, should he fail in that point, the balloon itself in the hands of a person of his ingenuity will probably perform at least as much as any hitherto executed'. An impatient Crosbie appealed directly to Charlemont for support. Charlemont was one of the founding members of the Royal Irish Academy, the commander-in-chief of the Irish Volunteers, and a widely respected promoter of the arts and science. He was no great lover of balloons, which he regarded as, 'silly inventions of a trifling age'. He later said that, 'every balloon but Crosbie's is odious to me.' In his letter, Crosbie was deferential and played the patriotic card, doubtless knowing of Charlemont's encouragement for all native scientific endeavours:

As the plan has already suffered much from delay, and I am warmly solicited to go to England immediately, I wish to get thro' my undertaking and make my first essay for fame in my native country. Many people have already subscribed and the work is in some forwardness; I therefore should be exceedingly hurt at my own disappointment, as well as feel most sensibly for the honour of my country in letting such a business drop, once they had embarked in it. To prevent this, therefore, my whole reliance was on your lordship, whose patriotic character would support it thro' an impartial trial, and whose numerous and respectable acquaintance, when having the honour of being solicited by your lordship, would not only assure to us the disposal of the necessary number of tickets, but expedite our experiments. I should think myself highly honoured in being allowed permission to send your lordship a few tickets for that purpose, and beg to know if it would be agreeable, as I should not take so great a liberty without previously acquainting your lordship. I have every apology to make for intruding so long on your lordship's time, but would not presume to do so if I did not flatter myself that the honour of this country was in this matter.

The claim that he was being invited to England may have been a stratagem, but if true, it confirms that Crosbie was in contact with persons or groups involved in ballooning there. There is no other direct evidence to support this, but there has been some speculation about the possibility, which is discussed at the end of this chapter. It is significant that Crosbie was already at the point of selling tickets in April 1784, but it was not until ten months later that his first manned flight took place.

Crosbie chose the fashionable Ranelagh Gardens as the location to exhibit his balloons. These had been opened in 1767 by Mr Hollister, an organ maker, and it was there that beaux and belles found entertainment and a suitable place to parade and promenade, to see and be seen. Hollister's gardens were modelled on those of the same name in London and comprised two and a half acres, with a temple, a lake and a burletta theatre for a band to play in. There were tea-rooms, garden parties, balls, musical recitals and firework displays, all patronised by ladies in powdered wigs and gentlemen with swords, some with stars on their coats to denote their ranks. The ladies wore hooped dresses with hinges on them to allow access through doorways and into carriages. The gardens would have been frequented too by the sots and gamesters, the bawds and jilts of Dublin's *demi-monde*. Mingling in the surrounds of such pleasure gardens in London and in Dublin was a way of breaking down the rigid social divide of other settings. They were also places of sexual dalliance, made more exciting by the secluded pathways, bowers, groves and alcoves. All kinds of attractions were provided, including, in 1777, a grand Venetian breakfast followed by a ball, and Hollister arranged to have the approach roads from the city to Ranelagh illuminated for night events. The scientist in Crosbie might not have been flattered at seeing 'tumblers, rope-dancers and balloon ascents' listed among the entertainments provided in Ranelagh. By 1784, the new Rotunda Gardens were beginning to challenge Ranelagh Gardens and, a year later, Hollister had decided to sell up. He had been singularly unlucky with the weather for many outdoor events, so much so that it was a standing joke in Dublin that he was jinxed. The great house in the gardens, Willbrook, was bought by the Carmelite Order of nuns in 1788, and their convent stood until the 1980s, when it was demolished for development. A small park still survives where the gardens once were.

On 16 August 1784, Crosbie unveiled his 'Grand Aeronautic Chariot' in Ranelagh Gardens. This 'aerial chariot' or 'flying barge' was intended to make a manned flight across the Irish Sea, referred to as St George's Channel. (Historically, this was the name given to the sea between Ireland and Wales, while nowadays, St George's Channel refers to a smaller area between Carnsore Point in Wexford and St David's Head in Wales.) A writer in the *Hibernian Magazine,* styling himself M.Y., was hugely enthusiastic:

After the approbation this curious machine has received from the learned and the ingenious and the general satisfaction it has given to all, we may be

Ranelagh Gardens. (© Dublin City Library and Archive.)

excused in pronouncing the invention of it to be one of the most remarkable efforts of human genius that has signalized itself in any country.

The article was accompanied by an image depicting a large balloon (or
envelope) and beneath it a sort of boat (called a car or gondola), with
masts, sails and a rudder-type object attached, and its design was attrib-
uted exclusively to Mr Crosbie. It also had two 'windmills' or *moulinets*,
one on either side. The writer gave a detailed description of the device,
noting that it displayed scientific, mechanical and nautical expertise:

The boat (or as the inventor calls it, chariot) which is to be carried into
the air by a balloon of forty feet in diameter filled with gaz, resembles

in some respect a boat or wherry with two masts; a pole runs out before from which to the top of the foremast is hoisted a triangular sail and one of the same figure, but something smaller, is spread from the after-mast by another pole or boom; the rudder is a light frame of wood covered with silk and of a considerable length which together with sails are managed with ease by the persons seated in the boat without altering the centre of gravity. On either side of the beam end is fixed a flyer exactly like a windmill which being turned round by an handle with such velocity that the leeward surface of the vanes, acting upon the air reverberated from the windward surfaces, forces the boat's sides against the wind and thereby permits the sails to collect sufficient power to carry it ahead. The same effect is produced on either side by simply turning the flyer a contrary way, and shifting the sails as in a ship. The chariot is made of a light frame of wood covered with thin silk or linen.

It was claimed that this 'Grand Aeronautic Chariot' of 36ft in length was constructed so as to allow it to be managed, 'with convenience to any point of the compass'. Crosbie was aware that some would say that his plan was impossible, but claimed to have conducted experiments in a stream of water which convinced him that the project was viable; the crucial issue was whether the balloon could indeed be directed in the air. He certainly succeeded in converting M.Y., who had gone to Ranelagh as a sceptic, but after interviewing Crosbie and seeing the machine for himself, was convinced that the aeronaut had at least 'half the compass at his command'.

Crosbie publicised his experiments by distributing handbills around the city. At first, his funding came from his own resources and subscriptions from the public. When these proved inadequate, he devised a plan to raise money by charging the public 2s 6d (half-a-crown) to view his experiments, as Lunardi also had done. Crosbie was always beset by financial problems, and even, 'with the utmost parsimony', he claimed that he had spent £500 of his own money on the whole project of his first flight, while receiving only £100 in subscriptions. He

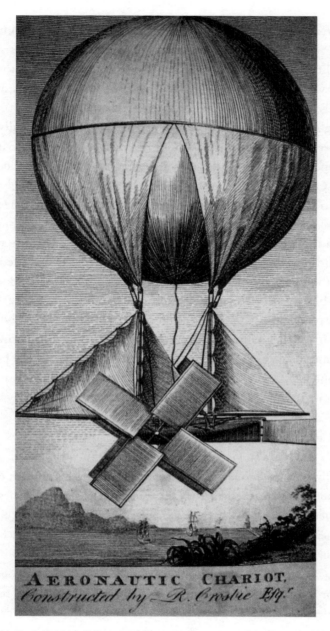

Richard Crosbie's balloon. *Hibernian Magazine*, 1784. (Courtesy of National Library of Ireland.)

was reported as suffering 'the severest mortification', disappointment and anxiety from the delays caused to his plans by the tradesmen he employed to make the apparatus. Mortification was an emotion with which he was to become very familiar over the next two years, and the word turns up with remarkable frequency in his writings.

During August 1784, Crosbie also set off a number of 'really curious' balloons of about 12ft in diameter on a daily basis. Public interest was sustained by frequent press coverage, and a writer who styled himself 'Don Quevedo' had a caustic letter in the *Freeman's Journal*, urging Crosbie to save money by using the pages of the *Hibernian Magazine* and the *Volunteer Journal* to line his balloon, advising that, as they were lighter and more inflammable in substance, and often in the clouds, they would soar like a kite. (The Montgolfier brothers had used paper lining in their early flights.) The flippant writer did not intend to ridicule Crosbie's efforts, and added a genuine tribute to his experiments as, 'a very practicable, ingenious attempt, in which he not only proves himself a great mechanic but a philosophical genius'. The terms 'philosophy' and 'science' were used as synonyms by writers of the period.

A second reader, Peter Wilkins, contributed another letter in the same vein in September, wittily satirising the politics of the day:

To Mr Crosbie at Ranelagh

Sir,

I perfectly agree with the ingenious Quevedo that you highly merit every public encouragement and applause for your philosophical researches and experiments; but as they have hitherto been only confined to speculative amusement I shall beg leave to convert them into real practical benefits to the public.

Your aeronautic chariot may be made the vehicle of the greatest good for this poor kingdom, and bring down peace, tranquility and content to our thoughtless and distracted politicians, who are neglecting their trade and manufactures, and are even regardless of their harvests, to patch and mend the constitution. My project is this: as every possible plan of reform which has whitherto been offered to the public has been found upon due consideration to be in some respect defective, and as it is not likely that a perfect one can be discovered in this globe of earth commonly called the world, I shall therefore propose that a balloon be formed of such uncommon magnitude as shall be able to ascend above the atmosphere of this globe of the earth. I imagine that a balloon of about the diameter of the Rotunda in Great Britain Street might answer the purpose. It should be covered with *Hibernian* and *Volunteer Journals*, as Quevedo mentions, and also with *General* and *Dublin Evening Posts*, as they likewise contain a vast quantity of inflammable matter.

To this balloon I would have an aeronautic chariot annexed, capable of containing four persons. This balloon should be doubly fortified with newspapers, and doubly varnished with the doubly blest oil of extreme unction, as it is to take an uncommon flight, far beyond which our earthly balloons have hitherto taken.

I propose, Mr Crosbie, that this balloon shall ascend to the moon and that the chariot shall convey thither the most respectable legislators and reformers of the state. The apparatus should be ready for flight against the meeting of that most august assembly the congress, on the 25th of October next. The 3rd day of their assembly (the 28th) is a full moon. Our state-menders are to be delegated by congress to the moon, in order to bring from thence an adequate plan of reform which may fully answer all the ends of mending our constitution removing our grievances, and totally eradicating all corruption from our senate. They would resemble the Decemviri, who were sent from Rome into Greece, to bring over with them the laws of that country.

But as our reformers are possibly unacquainted with the aerial road, I shall propose that two persons shall accompany them as guides, who can steer the balloon in the right course and I know no one so qualified for that important steerage as the earl of B-----l and Handy Pemberton Esq. who have been so long accustomed to lunar flights, vulgarly miscalled flights of lunacy. As this carriage will contain such invaluable personages, every precaution should be used to prevent accidents by the way, and particularly against the danger of fire from the immense quantity of inflammable air contained in the balloon. I would therefore have a very large vessel of holy water stowed in the chariot, and each person should have in his hand a brush or aspergas to sprinkle the balloon frequently with it ...

I also have another project for inflating this balloon with additional inflammatory gaz or foul air, in this manner. When the congress meets, let this balloon be placed in the centre of the field where they are assembled, then let each orator, when he is strongly moved by the spirit of liberality and freedom, instead of delivering his speech to the chairman, apply his mouth to the orifice of the tube of the balloon and deliver into that all his grievances of slavery, aristocracy, English influence, rotten boroughs, court corruption etc. etc. The aggregate body, with the affiliation of the Co. Galway delegates, will be able to fill a balloon of any magnitude ...

I think, Mr Crosbie, that if our project succeeds, we should be as well entitled to fifty thousand pounds apiece, as some others who have done less service to their country by their simple repeals.

I am Sir,
Your humble servant
Peter Wilkins.

The suggestion that an abundance of hot air was to be found in the speeches of politicians was one that appeared regularly in press comments. The political climate of the time was one of great debate on issues such as taxation, legislative independence, improved representation and relaxation of the Penal Laws against Catholics. A special congress was held in Dublin in October 1784 at which James Napper Tandy and Henry Flood were central figures, and the coincidence of this with Crosbie's experiments was seized upon by Wilkins and others.

By winter 1784, Dublin experienced the same 'ballomania' or 'balloonomania' that England did. The *Freeman's Journal* described 'the balloon influenza' which was raging in the city, 'Added to balloon hats, balloon bonnets, balloon caps, balloon ribbons, and balloon pins, the ladies now wear double balloon earrings and balloon side-curls, so that there are no less than seven balloon articles appertaining to the most beautiful balloon in nature – the head of a pretty woman!' Public interest in scientific endeavour had never been so widespread.

Crosbie's next launch from Ranelagh in early September was different in that it had a passenger: a cat in the basket attached to the balloon. 'An exceeding great concourse of people attended', reported the *Freeman's Journal*, and the balloon was visible for half an hour. 'This was the first balloon of any note exhibited in this kingdom', declared the *Hibernian Magazine*. In the basket was a note to the finder offering five guineas for information on where and when the cat was found, and in what condition. Previous descriptions of this event have noted that the cat's fate was not recorded, but in fact there is an account of his last breath. The balloon stayed aloft for two days and was seen passing over the coast of Scotland, but was blown back towards the Isle of Man and finished up in the sea, where a fisherman called Patrick McDermott came upon it. He thought it was 'some unknown and tremendous fish'. After observing the spectacle with astonishment, he and his crew eventually plucked up the courage to approach the balloon, and used a hook to penetrate it, whereupon:

> ...a considerable quantity of inflammable air rushed out in a stream of fire and with a great explosion. The terrors of the fishermen may now be better imagined than described. They fell flat upon their faces, trembling, groaning and howling. One exclaimed that it was the devil, another that it was the plague from Constantinople. 'Lord have mercy on us' says a third ... At length, Patrick McDermott, having crossed himself from head to toe, volunteered to stand erect and cry out 'In the name of God and the virgin Mary, what are you?' The poor cat that was sent up with the balloon and was just expiring went 'miaow' – flat went Patrick again on his face and gave vent not to his voice but to something less odoriferous. Half an hour later, courage prevailed and they took the balloon home in triumph.

At the launch of his next balloon, Crosbie was honoured by the attendance of the Duke and Duchess of Rutland. Rutland's appointment
as Viceroy in February 1784 coincided with Crosbie's declaration of
intent, and his support for the venture was hugely significant. His family
name was Charles Manners, and his wife was the noted beauty, Isabella
Somerset. This glittering couple presided over Irish society only for a
short period, from 1784 to 1787, but it was a time of great patronage
of the arts, of high living and excess. Rutland was said to have created a record for dining out that was never equalled by any subsequent
Viceroy. The couple's attendance in Ranelagh was a tremendous boost,
as they were a social magnet and added greatly to the drawing-power
of ballooning events. The Rutlands were highly popular and at the
centre of a hectic social scene in Dublin, chiefly perhaps because of
their lavish entertainments, and they behaved like royalty. The young
duke died of acute liver failure in 1787, aged only thirty-three. Crosbie
was fortunate to secure their patronage and it was a triumph for him
that the duchess released another of his balloons on 2 October 1784.
Admission to this event was 2s 8½d. It was reported that the balloon,
36ft in circumference, was visible for only nine minutes and nothing further was recorded about it. Later that month, the public was
informed that Crosbie's large balloon was 'in the greatest forwardness',
with the silk in the frames being varnished, and the apparatus being
attached. There were signs that financial support was not overwhelm-
ing, and newspapers encouraged people to support 'this ingenious
native' whom they had hitherto shamefully neglected.

Some people had reservations about Crosbie's model. A writer to
the *Freeman's Journal*, while supporting his plan and believing it was
achievable, had doubts about some aspects of it. He suggested that
Crosbie had been 'led away by his own ardour' in claiming that he
could travel at twenty leagues an hour, ten achieved by the wind and
ten by using the wings. The writer used scientific analysis to show that
in order to achieve this, 675 men would be required in the balloon, 'but
Mr Crosbie being but one man, we must not be disappointed if he do

Viceroy and Duke of Rutland, Charles Manners. *Hibernian Magazine*, 1784. (Courtesy of National Library of Ireland).

Duchess of Rutland, Isabella Somerset. *Hibernian Magazine*, 1784
(Courtesy of National Library of Ireland.)

not row so fast'. Nevertheless, the writer believed that Crosbie could achieve a channel crossing in five to six hours.

An unnamed rival was planning to send up a manned balloon in December: a report said that, 'a foreigner has for some weeks threatened to ascend from the Circus at Marlborough Street'. The language gives a very telling indication of the partisan attitude of the Dublin press at this time. This flight was in fact cancelled, and the people who had assembled to view it showed their frustration and disappointment by breaking into the grounds, threatening to destroy the whole apparatus. The report went on to say that Crosbie's balloon was now completed, and that he would certainly be ready for the appointed day, which was intended to be before the end of 1784. Bad weather affected the preparations, however, and Crosbie suffered from fatigue and 'a severe bilious attack which well nigh carried him off'. He persevered, giving directions from his sick bed, but the year ended without the achievement of a manned flight. The delays were stretching the patience of the public and Crosbie was obliged to place this prominent notice in the papers on 24-27 December:

Some material disappointments Mr. Crosbie has suffered in his work on account of the holidays, oblige him, though with the greatest reluctance, to defer his Aerial Experiment from RANELAGH until Tuesday next 4th January, when, if the weather permits, the public may rely on not having a second disappointment. He hopes that they may think an apology for the present one unnecessary, when he assures them his anxiety for the arrival of the day is much greater than can be felt by any other individual; and the mortification he suffers in being constrained to give this notice, much more severe than theirs can be in receiving it. The days being so short, the process for inflating the balloon will begin before seven o'clock in the morning, and it will be launched into the Atmosphere precisely at ten. As Mr. Crosbie's only view in imposing any tax on the public, is merely to defray the expense of this admirable Experiment and to gratify the greater number of his Countrymen, he has fixed the price of admission, to Non-subscribers, so low as Five Shillings British to the House and to the Gardens Half a Crown. Mr. Crosbie, on account of the early hour, had intended to have breakfast for such of his friends as should honour him with their presence at Ranelagh the morning of his embarkation – but on applying to Mr. Hollister was informed, it would be utterly impracticable, as from his house being so long shut up, he is not prepared for such an entertainment.

N.B. The balloon, now beautifully embellished, may be seen at the Rotunda every day, this week only, from eleven in the morning until three. Admission to Non-subscribers: One British Shilling.

Crosbie displayed his balloon in the Rotunda because it had an indoor exhibition space, which gave protection from the weather, and the arrangement was that the Lying-in Hospital would receive a quarter of the gate takings. This revenue was welcome to the hospital, which was in danger of bankruptcy at that time. All seemed set for a launch from Ranelagh on 4 January 1785. The Duke of Rutland played his part by ordering a number of revenue vessels to spread across the Irish Sea on the day of the flight, and this fleet had been augmented by merchant ships which volunteered their services 'for the same laudable and humane purpose'. There was a growing concern for the life of Richard Crosbie in his imminent undertaking, and a palpable sense of the immensity of the project:

A universal anxiety seems to pervade the public mind for the safety of Mr. Crosbie who is this day to undertake the boldest of enterprises by launching himself into the wide expanse of the atmosphere and to attempt to waft himself across the Irish channel. The element of the air is as yet but a new world to terrestrial travellers but this and future experiments may contribute possibly to noble discoveries with which the womb of time seems pregnant.

Another paper was more sceptical:

The whole sum added to science by this new mode of travelling is scarcely perceptible … All we can learn is that it is colder above the earth than on its surface and that the cold increases in proportion to the height to which the balloon rises – and this too was not unknown.'

The paper went on to urge 'plain common sense for the ears of the public in order to recover them from their delirium and prevent their being imposed on by bold assertions'. In what was to become an all too familiar sequence, the launch of 4 January was unsuccessful because of the weather. Crosbie was devastated, but the *Freeman's Journal* remained supportive, claiming that the failure was entirely due to circumstances outside his control. The following lampoon in the *Volunteer Journal* was a source of the greatest amusement, so much so that it was published three times in response to public demand. It was an entertaining piece of satire with many topical references, in a style that can still be appreciated today, even if many of the topical references are lost. One person received special mention, 'Aide-de-camps ushering in Peg Plunket and the great dignitaries of her chapter.' The same paper also mocked the hyperbole around the event and the frequent delays and cancellations of 'the day of all days':

'We hear that the mighty, monstrous, magnificent balloon will be floated in the air and carry its inventor over to London with a large piece of Irish tabbinet under his arm as a present for her Majesty – when??? … Millions unnumbered, men, women, children, infants of every age, gentle and simple, nobility and mobility, townsmen and gownsmen, wool-scribblers and paper-scribblers, captains of ships and captains of men, peace officers, war officers, custom house officers, counsellors and privy counsellors, gentlemen's gentlemen and gentlemen at large, ladies of easy virtue, lords of no virtue, barbers and surgeons (for they are now divided), volunteers, lads of the brush and of the comb, sheriffs, tarrers and featherers and attornies all joined together to see the wonderful air balloon at Ranelagh.

The Liberty Squadron mustered 9782 strong and 25000 weak, 1100 sailed

down the Poddle, the Dodder, the Grand Canal, the river of Stoneybatter
... The motley throng which for two hours before day and eight hours after
day beset the roads, the paths, the environs, the purlieus, the house-tops and
the backs of ditches impatient to see the Aerial Traveller's ascent.

Demme Jack, cries a wooden leg'd sailor, there's more fuss about this gal-
leon of theirs than about any we took last war! I wish he'd launch her and
let's see her build. – Oh! They're tin-plating her said a brazier's apprentice;
tin-plating said the tar, demme she's going such a voyage she ought to be
copper bottomed.

The children cried – for Crosbie's balloon could not ascend; the misses
tittered – for Crosbie's balloon could not ascend; their mamas scolded – for
Crosbie's balloon could not ascend. Some looked sullen, some looked sulky;
some laughed, some cried, and all were affected. 438 titled ladies fainted,
73 miscarried, nine of twins. Oh! Rutland, speedily add an increase to the
nobility, nor let the peerage of Ireland in the next generation suffer because
Crosbie's balloon did not ascend. Crack go the carriages, splash the horsemen, and coach meets coach and jostles in the dirt. Nine men transfixed by
the poles at the first news of the misfortune, 1932 drowned in the mud and
overwhelmed by wheels running over. 789 missing, dead – or dead drunk –
all thank God of the populace.

Mr. Foster's carriage has got entangled with the speaker's, Lord Earlsfort's
has deranged the Chancellor's. Confusion worse confounded! The
Secretary's wheel locked in with the Wicklow stage – 'Sdeath! Molyneux in
the mud – Oh! patriotism, where are thy stilts? Laugh, ye borough mongers,
heaven has declared against innovations. Laugh, ye rump-and-dozen citizens
who drowned the morning in sleep, the day in claret. Laugh, ye physicians
at the balloon fever which this day's unfettered curiosity has occasioned
– Crosbie's balloon could not ascend. The multitudes gazed without advantage, the nobles wished without effect. They retreated in disorder not like
the ten thousand under Xenophon, for Greece used no balloons, but following the balloon to the country where it first appeared, imitated the
conduct of the King of France whose 40,000 men on a formal occasion
'went up the hill and so came down again'.

Ranelagh Gardens today.

The *Freeman's Journal* lashed out at this attack on Crosbie, and claimed the writer was a hireling of one of Crosbie's rivals, a Scotsman named Dinwiddie. It urged the 'wretched hoary scribbler, the hired puffer of an itinerant philosophical lecturer [to] examine his own insignificance that never lifted him a foot above the humble clay he treads on.' The *Volunteer Journal* responded by publishing an even more ribald piece. With this piece was some doggerel, which mentioned by name many of those present. According to convention, only the first and last letters of some proper names were given. So, for example, the courtesan Peg Plunkett and her companion Sally Hayes are mentioned, as is Crosbie:

Jack Catch and Quill, P--g P------t too, attended by Miss H-----s.
Came with J-------e G ---------n in Mr. R--------s post-chaise.

Butchers brewers and bakers, in noddies with their wives
All swarmed from the town sir, as bees do from their hives,
And a fooling they did go.
Now Hollister the fortunate no doubt for sake of gain,
To give a second breakfast bespoke a show'r of rain
Then a-laughing he did go.
The C-------e comes to apologise (at least it has been told)
And owns that through confusion he melted all our gold
When inflating he did go.
He then concludes with what he feels and how acute his pain
For our great disappointment, but hop'd we'd come again,
When a-sailing he should go.
And now behold displeasure take place in every mind
When C-------e failed to fill his bladder full of wind
When inflating he did go.
The men enraged begin to curse, the frightened ladies pray,
A score of them miscarry and others faint away
Then groaning all do go.
And now comes honest P—k—t, that S---t of the S-----e,
Who'd take the odds he had not gaz a balloon to inflate
If sporting he would go.
He'd try'd it oft, she said, but ne'er could make it rise;
I therefore knew full well 'twould never mount the skies,
But a coining he would go.
Says one, what will become of this same grand balloon?
Why, it will make a nightcap just fit for the full moon,
If C------e will ever go.

It was soon after this disappointment of early January that Crosbie learned of the crossing of the English Channel by Jean Pierre Blanchard on 7 January. His dream of being the first man in history to complete a sea crossing by air was shattered. The *Hibernian Magazine* offered some consolation:

We would however recommend it to Mr Crosbie not to be disconcerted or unhappy at having lost the honour to be the first, as his undertaking, of which we have no reason to doubt the success, must be considered so far beyond any yet attempted, as to entitle him, when effected, to such a share of honour, as might be sufficient to gratify his warmest ambition.

As well as a place in history, Blanchard also gained a substantial monetary reward which Crosbie must have envied: he received 12,000 livres and a pension for life from King Louis XVI of France.

How much did Crosbie know of other aeronauts' achievements and specifically of Blanchard's balloon design and plan to cross the channel? How much of Crosbie's design was his own? How did he decide on the exact proportions and weights used in his experimental work? If he was influenced by developments in France and England, through what channels did he learn of these? Had he ever witnessed a balloon ascent? How did he source the materials required for a successful launch? These questions are difficult to answer because of lack of evidence. Certainly Crosbie had publicly identified the problem of navigation as the key issue at the beginning of 1784, possibly even before Blanchard had. Crosbie went further: he conducted experiments which have impressed at least one historian of early ballooning. J.E. Hodgson stated that Crosbie, 'appears to have been one of the first in the United Kingdom to examine with some thoroughness the problems involved in navigating balloons'. He refers to Crosbie's claim that he conducted experiments in a stream of water, and states that, 'he realized at an early date that sails fitted to a balloon were not analogous to sails as used in a boat, owing to the fact that a balloon moves wholly in one element while a boat moves in two elements of different density'. In discussing Blanchard's design, Hodgson refers to 'Richard Crosbie's slightly earlier idea of deriving a limited measure of dirigibility from the use of sails, both fixed and revolving.' This confirmation, from an authoritative source, that Crosbie's design was earlier than Blanchard's is a reliable indication of his originality and his place among the pioneers of flight, and justifies the Dublin press description of him as the discoverer of a method of balloon control. Ultimately, the development of proper dirigible balloons or airships would not be accomplished until another era of flight. Nevertheless, the *moulinet* or windmill is regarded as an early form of air-screw or propeller.

Crosbie's balloon showed many technical similarities to Blanchard's, but whether they came on these designs independently or were influenced by others is unclear. Blanchard used one *moulinet* or windmill where Crosbie used two, and Blanchard himself was accused of plagiarising the design from a M. Valet. It is worth taking a closer look at the sequence of events of early 1784, with regard to gondola design and attempts to navigate balloons. In his April 1784 letter to Charlemont, Crosbie wrote that he had made a model which he had shown to Dr Ussher and others. He referred to, 'the awkwardness of bringing such a thing thro' the streets', so it can be assumed to be a large-scale model. He also stated that his plans had 'already suffered much from delay' and that he was then, in April, at the point of selling tickets. Crosbie's own plans therefore were far advanced by April 1784, and it seems as if he was only short of money or proper materials in order to expedite matters. In going public with his announcement to the press on 7 February 1784, Crosbie must have had an advanced plan, ready to stand up to close scrutiny, and he had already won the support of the two Trinity Fellows whose names were attached: Ussher and Brown.

All this suggests that Crosbie must have developed his design by the end of 1783, or at the latest, by January 1784. In discussing Blanchard's design, Hodgson states that the earliest English design for a navigable balloon was that of Thomas Martyn, a natural-history draughtsman. Martyn first conceived the design in November 1783, apparently, but it was not published until October 1784. The first actual use of sails and windmill on a balloon in the air was by Blanchard on 16 October 1784. An image of Crosbie's unique aeronautic chariot was published in the *Hibernian Magazine* of September 1784, at which stage it was already on public exhibition. If only Crosbie had had the good fortune to have won the support of a man of means like Dr John Jeffries, he might well have achieved his ambition of becoming the first man to make a sea crossing in a balloon.

In some respects, Crosbie imitated the practices of other balloonists, for example by sending up animals first, by fundraising through subscription and by enlisting the press to achieve maximum publicity. He may also have known of the dimensions of the balloons and gondolas used by others, and learned from these. It is likely that very similar ideas were being generated by experimenters in different countries at the same time. Dr Barbara Traxler Brown has made a detailed study of the influences on Crosbie, and her research encompassed source material in French. She concludes that reports of European balloon experiments published in Dublin, and particularly in the magazine press, were an important source of information to him. In her view, Crosbie may have begun his experiments as early as October 1783. She suggests that Crosbie's eminent advisors in Trinity College may have had access to information on balloon developments through a network of contacts such as the Royal Society in London. Benjamin Franklin had been sending detailed reports of balloon developments in France to Joseph Banks in England, and Traxler Brown speculates that Crosbie might have had access to such information through his Trinity contacts. However, the fact that, in early April 1784, Crosbie met a group in Ussher's chambers in Trinity to explain his plan might suggest that, while supportive, they were not so closely involved in his work in the previous months. Crosbie certainly seems to have viewed that meeting as very important, as Charlemont had agreed to be guided by their conclusions, and Crosbie ensured that Ussher followed up with a letter to the earl. He was also very disappointed that a certain Mr Dean had not actually seen his model. This is the opening of Crosbie's letter of 13 April to Charlemont:

> I must entreat your lordship's pardon for again troubling you on the former subject, but as you were so kind as to say you would coincide, whatsoever might be the conclusion of Mr. Dean and Doctor Ussher, the inclosed letter

will give your lordship an idea of the opinion of the latter (who is particularly cautious) can venture to give to the world. I have not had the satisfaction of shewing the model I made to Mr. Dean, as he was engaged on the evening of our meeting about some law business, and could not come to my house where the model was exhibited to the other gentlemen and to doctor Ussher, all of whom seemed vastly pleased with it. From the awkwardness of bringing such a thing thro' the streets, I have had the mortification not to be able to shew it to Mr. Dean, whose good opinion would stamp so much credit on it.

Traxler Brown identifies several factors influencing Crosbie's successful promotion of his plan: the existence of 'a spectator public for scientific phenomena', the support of influential figures such as Charlemont, and the spirit of national pride that a native Irishman was at the forefront of a unique experiment. Her conclusion is that the critical factor in the success of the enterprise was, 'Crosbie's own fundamental ability and sustained commitment to scientific and technical experimentation.'

This conclusion seems inescapable. Crosbie showed an amazing engineering ability in successfully experimenting with all the technical requirements of designing and constructing a large balloon in such a short timeframe. He had to procure and pay for many yards of silk of suitable quality, find artisans capable of stitching the gores or strips together effectively, and workshops large enough to cope with the amount of material needed for the envelope. He had to make or buy a varnish which would provide an effective seal over the silk. A contemporary recipe for varnish is found in the Poynton Collection in the Royal Aeronautical Society, and cited by L.T.C. Rolt. It shows how much specialised knowledge of materials and procedures was required to construct a reliable balloon, 'To one gallon of linseed oil add 2oz of litharge, 2oz of white vitriol and 2oz of gum-sanderick. Boil for an hour over a slow fire. When cool strain off and mix with 1½ oz of turpentine.'

Crosbie must have had a good knowledge of chemistry, at a time when information about the properties of gases and acids was rudimentary. He was an entrepreneur who had to persuade influential figures

Lord Charlemont. (Courtesy of
Public Record Office of Northern
Ireland.)

that his project was viable; he had to secure the capital required and find
imaginative ways of promoting the launch event and ways of enticing the
public to part with money. Crosbie seems to have had responsibility for
transporting the balloon back and forth across the city, from Ranelagh
to the Rotunda, and for ensuring that there was an efficient system of
generating hydrogen and conveying it to the envelope. He was a scientist
and a showman, a romantic and an idealist, an enthusiast and an obsessive,
a man infused with a spirit of derring-do, who dreamed of things that
never were and asked 'Why not?' In short, Richard Crosbie was a genius.

Above all, he was an optimist. Despite losing the race to be the first
to cross the sea, Crosbie was undeterred. He continued to plan for a
manned ascent from Ranelagh, and announced that the event would
be heralded by firing guns at different quarters of the city as a signal
to people to assemble, in the certainty of seeing an ascent. The public
would not be disappointed on the next occasion. When it came, all the
accoutrements of windmills, sails and rudders were simply left behind
on the ground. Maybe Crosbie had by then lost faith in their efficacy,
and even without them, he rose magnificently to the occasion.

THE FIRST MANNED
FLIGHT IN IRELAND

Who can say these are not stirring times?

Volunteer Journal

The next date set for Crosbie's flight from Ranelagh was 19 January 1785. The *Volunteer Journal* was giddy with anticipation, 'Wonderful will be the bustle and confusion of the week – Congress meets–Parliament meets– term begins–and Crosbie ascends with his balloon. Who can say these are not stirring times?' Shopkeepers and householders were advised to be especially vigilant as, with so many people heading for Ranelagh, there would be rich pickings for thieves and vagabonds in premises around the city. It was reckoned that business would be boosted:

> By Saturday next, the city of Dublin will contain more inhabitants than were ever in it at one time; nor does Mr. Crosbie's aerial voyage add few to the number as we find that the expectation of a sight so uncommon has drawn a considerable number of people who have no other business.

Dublin was accustomed to seeing the annual review of the Volunteers in their resplendent uniforms, but there were no precedents for the kind of public entertainment which Crosbie was to put on. The tradition of 'riding the franchises' was the nearest equivalent. This festive event took place every three years on 1 August, and brought huge numbers onto the streets to watch a colourful cavalcade of public representatives, tradesmen and manufacturers. It was led by the Lord Mayor and the purpose was to mark the boundaries of city limits. Master craftsmen, journeymen and apprentices of all the trade guilds paraded in full regalia, many of them on horseback. There were platforms or floats with people dressed in costumes appropriate to the trade. To Dubliners, the event was known as 'riding the fringes' and there was general regret when the custom ended around the late 1780s.

Crosbie's launch, however, was a one-man show in comparison to this. Moreover, it combined spectacle and science, innovation and danger, education and entertainment in an unprecedented way. Never before was a scientific innovation so much debated in the coffee houses and in the streets of Dublin. This was the age of the enlightenment, an age of wonder and progress, an age of limitless possibility. All over Europe, old ways were being challenged, new ideas and inventions were emerging and new directions being explored in many aspects of public life, politics, literature and science. This added greatly to the sense of new frontiers being explored by intrepid aeronauts abroad and at home.

Crosbie was supported by a committee which managed practical arrangements for the day's events. Its members included George Ogle, William Caldbeck, William Downes, Oliver Carlton, Revd Dr Ussher, Richard Cuthbert, Revd Mr Ledwich, John Macauley, William B. Dunn and Mr Crosthwaite. Lord Charlemont, and the Duke of Leinster were also in attendance. A traffic plan was devised, which obliged all carriages to continue to Milltown after dropping off passengers, and no carriages were to be allowed to stand between Northumberland Street and Coldblow Lane (now Belmont Avenue). The time fixed at first was 10a.m. but at the request of the Fellows of Trinity College it was changed to 11a.m. to facilitate students who were sitting exams. Twelve rounds of cannon were to be fired at various points around the city – Ranelagh, Thomas Street, St Stephen's Green, and Marlborough Green – to alert the citizenry.

Newspapers recorded crowds of at least 20,000; Hodgson claims 40,000, while the *Freeman's Journal* made the grandiose claim that there, 'could not be less than 150,000 spectators'. (In fact, the population of the city was probably only about 180,000 at that time.) It rained heavily the night before, and the preparations took far longer than anticipated. Crosbie showed alarming signs of anxiety and distress all morning, with good reason, as he could ill-afford to disappoint the volatile crowd yet again. From daybreak, work went on producing hydrogen, using large quantities of water, sulphuric acid, iron filings and/or zinc. At the last minute, it was decided to drop the windmill device and sails, on the realisation that they were too heavy. This was a major adaptation, and perhaps an acknowledgement by Crosbie that they were superfluous items of equipment. The main priority was to ensure that the balloon would rise, with its load of ballast, scientific equipment, other supplies and a heavy passenger. By afternoon, all advice to Crosbie was to abandon any attempt to cross the sea, and simply to aim for a short flight.

The process of generating hydrogen and conveying it to the envelope was quite elaborate and challenging in itself. In France, Professor Charles had first used a chest of lead-lined drawers for the process, but this proved cumbersome and was soon abandoned. Instead, he used a number of barrels which were arranged in a circle and connected to a central larger barrel which was connected to the envelope. I have found no clear description of how Crosbie worked, but it is certain that he used a process similar to that of Charles, as this quickly became standard. The question of how exactly Crosbie might have learned about this method remains unresolved. The system was as follows: hydrogen was generated in each barrel in turn by adding water and sulphuric acid to iron filings or zinc. The exact quantities of water, acid and iron or zinc would have been determined by Crosbie himself by trial and error. Tiberius Cavallo was one of the earliest writers on the science of aerostation, and in his book published in 1785, he stated that a balloon of 30ft in diameter, with a capacity of 14,137 cubic feet, would require 3,900lbs of iron turnings, 3,900lbs of vitriolic acid and 19,500lbs of water. Another book, from 1823, *Aeronautica or Voyages in the Air* (no author given) had the following instructions:

> The vitriolic acid must be diluted by five or six parts water. Iron may be expected to yield in the common way 1,700 times its own bulk of gas: or one cubic foot of inflammable air to be produced by 4½ ounces of iron, the like weight of oil of vitriol and 22½ ounces of water. Six ounces of zinc, an equal weight of oil of vitriol and 3 ounces of water are necessary for producing the same amount of gas. It is more proper to use the turnings or chippings of great pieces as of cannon &c, than the filings of that metal, because the heat attending the effervescence will be diminished.

The same book says that Lunardi filled his balloon using about 2,000lbs of iron, 2,000lbs of vitriolic acid and 12,000lbs of water. It is clear that, like his fellow aeronauts, Crosbie would have been dealing with massive amounts of these substances, at a time when the only previous experiments with them would have been done in minute quantities and in laboratory conditions. How and where he acquired these materials, and how much he paid for them are questions that are impossible to answer. The length of time it would take to generate a sufficient amount of the gas to ensure that the balloon would lift was another variable, and had to be learned by experience. This inevitably meant frequent long delays and some ultimate disappointments for the waiting crowds, so that, as well as dealing with volatile substances, Crosbie (and other early balloonists) also had to deal with volatile crowds.

There is a good description of the inflation process in Charles Coulton Gillispie's book of 1983. The hydrogen was produced in each small barrel and conducted into the central container, and from there into the envelope. When the iron in one barrel was exhausted, the flow of acid would be passed to the next barrel in the circle and so on. This allowed time for cooling and recharging each barrel in turn. At first, each barrel was connected to the central unit by a pipe of tinned iron, but a lead pipe soon replaced this. These became very hot in the process and they had to be wrapped with wet cloths. Through these pipes the vapour travelled to the central trough, which was covered, where it was washed through water. This cut out some of the spasms and excessive heat that were encountered at earlier attempts. Finally, the gas travelled by pipe to the limp envelope, which gradually rose as it filled. It was always very difficult then

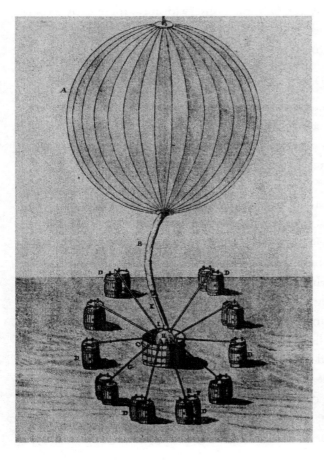

Process of filling hydrogen balloon. (Courtesy of Princeton University Press).

to decide on the best moment to declare the balloon ready for release.

The early experiments of Professor Charles and the Robert brothers required cool heads and an ability to improvise. Hydrogen at first emerged spasmodically and belched into the balloon in huge waves. The reaction in the barrel produced such intense heat that the water could vapourise and pass into the balloon with the hydrogen. Then it condensed and formed drops of sulphuric acid at the bottom of the envelope. These drops could easily burn through the fabric if they were not quickly shaken off. The connecting pipes and the balloon itself became very hot during the process and had to be cooled with wet cloths and sprays of water. Gillispie's observation on these early experiments of Charles and the Robert brothers seems equally applicable to Crosbie in Ranelagh:

> In a small enclosed courtyard in a densely populated section of the city, a handful of largely inexperienced people were collecting an unprecedented quantity of the most inflammable gas known through a tube too hot to touch into the confinement of a rubberized bag that was close to catching fire if it was not first chewed through by sulphuric acid.

Professor Charles had led the way in discovering best practice in filling a balloon, but he had the weight of the French Academy behind him and it is believed that the great chemist Lavoisier was secretly advising him. Richard Crosbie had no such august body or individual at his shoulder, unless perhaps his Trinity advisors, and probably discovered the best methodology largely by his own experiments. This makes his achievements even more astonishing.

The Ranelagh balloon was adorned with paintings of Minerva, goddess of wisdom, and Mercury, messenger of the gods, enveloping the arms of Ireland, and with symbols of the winds. Illustrations confirm that his flying barge or aerial chariot had simply become a basket without any attachments. This Latin motto was inscribed on the balloon: *Prapetibus pennis acerus se credere caelo.* It was a quotation from Virgil's

Process of inflating
envelope: on left
Montgolfiere balloon,
on right Charliere
balloon. (Courtesy of
the Board of Trinity
College Dublin.)

Aeneid, which translates as, 'He dared to trust his life to the sky, float-
ing off on swiftly driving wings'. The reference was to the story of
Daedalus fleeing from Minos, 'towards the cold stars of the north, the
Greater and Lesser Bears, by a route no man had ever gone before'.
Perhaps it was tempting fate to refer to the story of Daedalus and
Icarus, which ended in disaster, but this does not seem to have been a
worry. It was described as a sphere of 34ft in diameter, with a capac-
ity of 20,579 cubic feet and capable of lifting 1286lbs. (However, the
Hibernian Magazine of 1784 had claimed that the balloon was 40ft in
diameter.)

Crosbie went on board his 'chariot' at 1p.m. but found, 'to his mortification', that it would not rise. More hydrogen was added, and Crosbie
finally achieved his aim of being the first man to ascend in a balloon
in Ireland at 2.40p.m. Using his speaking trumpet, he gave orders for
rockets to be fired as a signal. As the moment approached, 'ecstatic
pleasure brightened his countenance and beamed in sparkling lustre
from his eye'. When lift-off was finally achieved, a solemn silence fell
on the assembly and then, 'he mounted awfully majestic, while the air
resounded with the shouts, the prayers, the admiration of the delighted
multitude'. The flamboyant showman in Crosbie made the most of the

theatre of the occasion: he was dressed in a robe of oiled silk lined with white fur, his waistcoat and breeches were made of quilted satin, and he wore Moroccan boots and a Montero cap (or turban) made from leopard skin. 'When he found himself ascending, a spring of ecstatic joy appeared to animate his countenance.'

The sheer grandeur and elegance of the sight was deeply moving and inspiring. People who had before gazed up at the clouds and at the birds, at the stars and at the storms, and imagined the gods in their heavens, now gazed up at what they could never have imagined possible. Descriptions of the event convey the sense of awe and astonishment at the achievement, and it takes a leap of imagination to understand

Contemporary illustration of Crosbie's ascent from Ranelagh Gardens. (© Dublin City Library and Archive.)

the impact of the ascent on the mesmerised throng, as reported in Faulkner's *Dublin Journal*:

Mr Crosbie's experiment yesterday proves his genius is as great as his intrepidity; a trial was made till between 8 and 9 o'clock in the morning with filings of iron to fill the balloon, but from its bad quality and consequent slowness of solution, was the cause of considerable delay; from the time Mr Crosbie ordered to charge with zynck, the process went on with desired success, and about half past two o'clock he took his aerial flight, amid the concourse of at least 20,000 spectators. Idea cannot form anything more aweful and magnificent than his rise; he ascended almost perpendicular, and when at a great height, seemed stationary. He was but three and a half minutes in view, when he was obscured by a cloud. It was agreed upon by his particular friends, as the wind was from the SE and being late in the day, that when he cleared the city he should descend as soon as possible, accordingly by means of his valve, he let himself down near Clontarf, and fulfilled every engagement and expectation that the public, his friends and those who have the honour of his acquaintance always formed of him ... No man ever undertook such a perilous voyage with so much cheerfulness, and we are doubly happy that no accident has happened to this enterprising youth, nor can we doubt a moment of his original plan to cross the channel succeeding, and thereby prove to the World that Ireland in scientific knowledge is not inferior to any part of it.

This is the *Freeman's Journal* account:

The report of the cannon roused the whole town; company of the first fashion speedily rattled away to Ranelagh in their carriages and indescribable crowds of horse and foot, gentry, citizens etc. hastened to the curious and awful scene. By 11 o'clock the Garden was immensely thronged with gentlemen and ladies, and the surrounding fields with tens of thousands of spectators ...

At twenty-five minutes before three, a most beautiful solemn and

The flamboyant hero. *Hibernian Magazine*, 1785. (Courtesy of National Library of Ireland.)

wonderful sight took place. The balloon ascended with its courageous master, slow, perpendicular and majestic, but soon increasing its velocity, rose above the clouds and was out of sight in three minutes and a half. Repeated shouts of applause were sent to the sky to cheer the brave adventurer who kept waving a speaking trumpet he had in his hand as long as he remained in sight. When lost to the view of the many thousands of spectators, effusions of prayer and exclamations of good wishes for his safety were heard around ...

No man ever showed greater courage than did Mr Crosbie yesterday, in order to gratify public curiosity. His only fear seemed to be that of disappointing the expectations of myriads of people who attended to see his exhibition. Distress for this reason painted his countenance till his balloon was liberated but when he found himself ascending a spring of exstatic joy appeared to animate his whole frame, and the MAN shone forth him in all the pride of intrepidity. Yet did he seem perfectly collected, exhibiting a noble and shining picture of a real philosopher and a real hero.

1985 Commerative stamp designed by Robert Ballagh. (By kind permission of An Post)

When he disappeared from view after four minutes, a cannon was fired to signal so to him. As he had heard that he might experience deafness, one of his first actions was to shout, and he was pleased to hear his voice echoing in the clouds. At the highest point, 'the scene was astonishing and glorious, the sun in unknown splendour in the expanse of deepest blue, and the clouds rolling beneath his feet'. He was likened to, 'a feathered Mercury or some angel sailing on the bosom of the air'. He might be said to have experienced what the poet Browning described as 'the first fine careless rapture' as he enjoyed for the first time in Irish history a bird's-eye view of the world. The most immediate sensation he experienced was of absolute silence and apparent stillness that other aeronauts had reported on in England and France.

Reports claimed that he reached a height of about 18,000 feet, and with his barometer showing a decrease of pressure to 13.5 inches, Crosbie heeded the advice of friends and opened a valve to allow him to descend. Another account says that, at his highest point, the barometer reading was 15 inches 99 hundredths, and states that this was equivalent to two Irish miles. These claims must be grossly exaggerated, and reflect the difficulty people had in describing the unprecedented event. The balloon passed over Poolbeg lighthouse, and as he lost height, Crosbie first heard a dog barking and then the noise of ship-carpenters, which, after the absolute silence of the skies, was dramatic. He threw out a grappling hook, and the rope was held fast by people below, who assisted in landing him safely at the North Strand, 'near the island of Clontarf'. A large crowd gathered and carried him shoulder high in his aerial chariot, with the balloon floating over it, to the home of Lord Charlemont in Rutland Square (now the Hugh Lane Gallery in Parnell Square). The cortège followed a route via Summerhill, Britain Street and Granby Row. What a spectacle it must have provided. Next day, 'the triumphant hero who made the air subservient to his wishes' received a generous gift of £200 from the Lord Lieutenant. According to the currency converter of the British National Archives, this would have the spending worth of approximately €14,000 or £12,000 today.

Another contemporary source confirms newspaper reports. *Watson's Almanack and Directory* of 1786, under the heading 'Historical Annals of the City of Dublin', recorded the Ranelagh flight as the main event of 1785, describing Crosbie as, 'the first person who explored the Irish atmosphere'and stating that he landed on the North Strand near Marino. The acclaim of Dublin was expressed in ballads which soon appeared on the streets, such as this one on the day after the flight, predicting that the Irishman would rule the waves as well as the skies:

Aspiring youth who with Montgolfier vies
To scale the crystal palace of the skies
Whose infant genius spawned the noble thought
Which man adult hath to perfection brought,
How must thy breast 'twixt hope and fear be torn
When thou uplifted from the earth art borne,
And stands within that awful space above
Earth's glorious canopy, the seat of Jove.
The bold Leander crossed the Hellespont
And safely swam the tempestuous tide along.
More daring thou who tempts the dangerous seas

Charlemont House. (© Dublin City Library and Archive.)

Sans earth or water but the gentle breeze.
There in the annals of eternal fame
Thyself shall see the gods inscribe thy name,
And lightly mounted on the wings of air,
Like a new sun, shall gild the hemisphere.
May thy attempts with quick success be crowned
To outstrip thy rivals on Brittanic ground,
Where envy shall her inflamed malice shroud
And Ixion-like shall but embrace a cloud.
'Tis destined now Hibernia's favoured son
Shall do what man as yet hath never done:
Wrest that great boast from Albion's haughty throne,
And rule the empire of the seas alone.

A long poem entitled *The Aerial Voyage* was published on 24 January, with an introduction which declared that:

> ... in common with the aerial traveller himself, and with every feeling spectator in that immense crowd, we have experienced the most grateful benevolent and sublime sensations ... Thus in the field of experimental disquisition Mr. Crosbie's dauntless spirit hath secured him unrivalled pre-eminence; and to the great ornament of our universe, our country, of science and of human nature, a grateful nation will look up for discoveries of the highest import ... While this gentleman stands so deservedly high in the esteem and admiration of a discerning people ever ready to patronize native genius, may these lines perpetuate the private respect, gratitude of an individual scarcely known to Mr. Crosbie, yet a warm admirer of his transcendent merit.

This encomium captures the high regard in which Crosbie was held immediately after the Ranelagh flight. A note with the poem gave the information that Crosbie had first conceived of the idea of a balloon flight as early as 1773. This claim is intriguing, and is easy to dismiss as hyperbole, but it may perhaps be true that Crosbie speculated about flight even then, the year in which he entered Trinity. We know enough of his intrepidity and ingenuity to indicate that he could certainly have contemplated the possibility of human flight during his college days.

The poem itself was equally effusive about Crosbie's achievement, as the following extract shows. There was a special note of national pride that, 'contending states shall own/ th'idea ours, the glory all our own.' (The 'patriot throne' in the lines below is the home of Lord Charlemont, 'the volunteer earl'):

So, social glides the victor chief along
Eyed as a deity by half the throng
While gathering thousands guard his passage home,
And waft triumphant to the patriot throne.

Hail Crosbie! To thy research is giv'n
To explore the trackless space twixt earth and heaven.

In earlier lines, the scene at Ranelagh on 19 January is described:

A motley, strange and miscellaneous throng,
These for reform and those against it strong,
A single day suspends discordant aims,
Turn'd from low politics to higher themes;
All to the garden, garters, rags and stars,
On foot, on horse, in hack or glittering cars.
All emulous who first shall gain th'approach,
Here rolls the chariot, here the blazon'd coach.
But lo, ere yet the lusty morning dawns
The state's array invests the circling lawns.

A moment now, to love, to friendship due,
Soft from the crowd the anxious chief withdrew,

Illustration by Tom McCormack.

But buskin'd soon, in drawers, satin vest,
An ample stole and graceful turban drest,
Again returns all dauntless to the charge
Smiles on us all and mounts his airy barge.

('The state's array' refers to the two regiments of infantry, a squadron of horse and part of the train of artillery which was in attendance at Ranelagh.)

There have been claims of a flight from Navan, Co. Meath, which preceded Crosbie's. These are based on a report in Faulkner's *Dublin*

Journal of a M. Rosseau (sometimes cited as Rousseau) who took off in a balloon from Navan on 15 April 1784 with a ten-year-old drummer boy as a companion. There was enough detail in the account to make it plausible, including the information that people could hear the drummer boy playing 'The Grenadier's March' for fifteen minutes after the balloon took off. They were said to have landed in a field near Ratoath, and the boy to have received a bump on the head as he leapt from the basket. However, in a letter to *The Irish Times* on 17 April 1984, Richard Hawkins of the Royal Irish Academy stated that the story was a hoax perpetrated by the editor of the *Dublin Evening Post*, John Magee. Hawkins cited the authority of the British Aeronautical Society. The hoax succeeded too well, so much so that the story of Rosseau's fictional flight has been repeated many times. Another inaccurate claim is that Crosbie's first flight was from Leinster House; he did ascend from there, but it was six months after Ranelagh. Many accounts of Crosbie's career err in conflating details from different flights, and the commemorative plaque in Ranelagh Gardens wrongly refers to a hot-air balloon rather than a hydrogen balloon.

After Ranelagh, Crosbie's plans took on a greater momentum. He dutifully took pains to thank the nobility and gentry for their support and said that his next effort would bring, 'that universal satisfaction which he so much wishes'. He said that he was planning a second voyage, this time with a companion, whom he did not name. He promised that he would also expand the hydrogen-generating apparatus to ensure that inflation could be completed in two hours, and he would restore the wings. The balloon was damaged in a storm at the Rotunda Gardens two days after his flight, but it had been repaired and he said that it would be on show again. He was engaged in making a new balloon which would be, 'the most perfect and most elegant yet constructed in any kingdom'. He was also reported to be working in collaboration with the astronomer Dr Ussher of Trinity College who would make 'earthly observations' while Crosbie added his aerial discoveries.

A Mr Harding of Meath Street set off a balloon near Dolphin's Barn, specifically to demonstrate that Crosbie's plan to cross the Irish Sea was feasible. On St Patrick's Day, a Montgolfiere balloon was released from St Stephen's Green, with the inscription, 'Thus we rise to fame and glory.' Unfortunately, the fire spread from the furnace to the envelope, and the whole thing was destroyed. 'Thus it ended like all schemes for the real benefit of Ireland, hitherto liberated, *in fumo*,' observed the *Dublin Journal*.

Nor was Crosbie short of advice. One person wrote that he should use Kilkenny coal, as its sulphurous and light vapour would be better than the 'noxious effluvia' of his usual method. (In fact coal-gas did have many qualities which made it suitable for balloons and it was used in the nineteenth century, but it was not as light as hydrogen.) Crosbie was also advised that his balloon would absorb water and become heavier as it travelled over the sea, and since he 'had nothing to do with entertaining the fishes' he should forget about sea crossings. He could instead become the 'letter carrier of the nation' if he converted his balloon to 'an inland aerial packet' which would defy bad roads and robbers. Yet another ingenious idea was that invalids could be raised up to breathe a purer air and travel without the discomfort and jolts of a country road.

It seemed to be roses, roses all the way for Crosbie as 1785 advanced; he had joined an elite corps of fliers who had observed their world from a perspective never before known to man. The accolades rang in his ears as he looked towards his next attempt at crossing the Irish Sea. Accolades, however, would not pay his bills, and he must have been very grateful to the Duke of Rutland for his gift of £200. In December 1784, Crosbie had informed the public that he had already spent £500 on his preparations, but had only received £100 in subscriptions; the final cost of the Ranelagh flight was possibly as high as £900. The citizens of Dublin soon realised that a balloon could be observed from anywhere in the city, and all they would miss would be the excitement of the actual lift-off, or sometimes, the tedium, delay, and disappointment.

❦ 6 ❧

THE STUDENT HERO
OF ROYAL BARRACKS

This manoeuvrer seems to imagine he has a
patent for playing on the credulity of the town ...
and rendering the metropolis idle day after day.

Freeman's Journal

Crosbie's next attempt at a sea crossing was in May 1785, and the location was Palatine Square, Royal Barracks (now Clarke Square in the
National Museum of Ireland at Collins Barracks.) The event was heralded in Faulkner's *Dublin Journal* during April, with an assurance that
there would be no delay or disappointment on this occasion. With a
performer's instinct, Crosbie fixed his flight for Ascension Thursday, 5
May, but was then over-ruled by his committee, which changed it to
the following Tuesday, 10 May.

The price for entry was now 5s 5d, directly as a result of his losses
at Ranelagh and his recent expenses. A traffic plan was outlined in the
Volunteer Journal of 9 May: carriages were to go down Barrack Street

Clarke Square, National Museum at Collins Barracks, formerly Palatine Square, Royal Barracks.

(now Benburb Street), set down their passengers at the gate, and go on towards the park on Arbour Hill, so that the traffic would flow smoothly. The Barracks square was regarded as an excellent venue because of 'the capacious corridors and galleries to every floor of the buildings commanding the most extensive view'.

However, the attempt of 10 May was a total failure and Crosbie felt the full force of public anger, learning a hard lesson about the fickleness of fame, the fury of the mob and the venom of the press. His erstwhile ardent supporter, the *Freeman's Journal*, carried one particularly scathing report, saying that 'the aerial adventurer should not have named the particular day and hour without an absolute or moral certainty of gratifying the public'. Their report also excoriated the class of person to whom the event appealed:

> Thousands on thousands were seen running, walking, hobbling, grunting and creeping through all the streets, lanes and alleys of this city to occupy every field and vacant space that could afford a front, side or back prospect of an ascent to, or above the clouds ... The borders of the river were lined with

multitudes thick as grasshoppers at the decline of the day when the falling of fragrant dews animate and inspire their song. Not an empty spot to be discerned in the environs of the Barracks ... Here a range of coaches, there a set of demi-reps, and upstart quality, with clean petticoats and shirt-sleeves, white stockings, good shoes putting the best foot foremost. In another group might be observed an inferior order of females whose bloated faces and half-extinguished eyes added to a taudry and mean appearance might induce us to imagine them partridges ... a covey broken loose from the greasy and foetid stews in the neighbourhood of the Blind Quay ...

In a word, the various and mixed ranks of every species of people who inhabit the metropolis, or some miles round, who lost their day, their work and their wages to see what even the eyes of Argus, though one hundred in number, could not see, were truly astonishing ... The whole city and country, being thus, as the vulgar proverb says, brought to bed of disappointment, withdrew in reluctant multitudes to their respective homes, where each found his loss, in a fruitless absence of several tedious hours from business or pleasure.

Crosbie issued a handbill after this disappointment which only irked the paper more:

Instead of a modest and respectable address which the public thought to have seen yesterday from the balloon schemer as an apology for disappointing 100,000 persons of seeing him rise on Tuesday last like a lanthorn tied to the tail of a paper kite were they insulted with a low, vulgar and dissatisfactory handbill distributed through the streets by shoeblacks. This manoeuvrer seems to imagine he has a patent for playing on the credulity of the town and of doing the great and irreparable injury of rendering the metropolis idle day after day to the loss of many thousands of £ sterling from neglect of business. Whether he ascends this day or any other day seems now a matter of much indifference, since through vain boasting, want of abilities, or at least want of attention, he has descended so much in general opinion as to put it out of the power of any future success to re-instate himself in public estimation.

The *Freeman's Journal* acknowledged that Crosbie's intrepidity was unquestionable, but was disillusioned with ballooning in general, 'a pursuit that has yet answered no one salutary purpose to mankind, and most probably never will'. Crosbie was advised that he 'had not yet maturely digested his information, so as to enable him to reduce his knowledge to an accuracy of practice'. Crosbie had made two attempts on Tuesday 10 May, and both failed, claimed the paper, because he 'had lulled himself into a supineness, from too vain a conception of his skill in the process and too much boasted a confidence of success'.

The paper turned its favour on his rival, a Frenchman named Potain, who was planning a flight in June, and it advised Crosbie to learn from Potain's methods. The *Volunteer Journal* also attacked Crosbie as being, 'deficient in modesty or abilities,' and rejected his excuses, declaring that 'no person should call out 50,000 at a great expense with positive assurances of entertainment and then assign reasons in excuse'. Since no flight took place, one reporter chose to admire the ladies, noting that, 'there never was seen in this kingdom or perhaps in any other, such a noble and charming collection of females, great and small'. Crosbie's explanation for the failure was that a quantity of air was already in the balloon and did not allow enough hydrogen (inflammable air) into it. The 'philosophers of Meath Street' commented that 'our Barrack philosopher' held back on the use of inflammable air, 'owing to his kind recollection that the air of this kingdom was sufficiently inflamed already'. There was also speculation that the large numbers in such a small enclosed space, 'so rarified the circumambient air that its medium was as light as the inflammable air within the balloon'.

Crosbie's desperation at the failure of his plans can be sensed in his reported vow that he would 'either ascend or die' in another attempt on 12 May at the same location. This is an indication of the pressure from the media and from public expectation which obliged many of the early balloonists to launch without thorough preparation. The events were so crowded, with people often in a confined space, that a riot was always a possibility after a long, frustrating wait. Crosbie had lost a great deal of his raw materials on 10 May and these had to be replaced very quickly; the fact that he was ready to try again just two days later shows his determination, and he must once again have been under considerable personal strain over those days.

There were chaotic scenes at the Barracks on Thursday 12 May as the balloon was being readied. The Duke and Duchess of Rutland, Lord Charlemont and the Duke of Leinster were in attendance. Crosbie now experienced an unforeseen problem: his own weight. Before he stepped in, the basket was already laden with twelve stone of ballast in twelve bags, a grapple, a rope, a fly, a thermometer, a speaking trumpet, a compass, a basket of provisions and an instrument to measure altitude which hung from the basket. All of these instruments were considerably larger than their modern equivalents, and the last one mentioned was probably designed by the scientist Richard Lovell Edgeworth.

After several efforts, the portly Crosbie eventually had to accept that he was simply too heavy – six stone too heavy by one account – to be lifted in the basket. Crosbie's weight was estimated at 224lbs or sixteen stone. The crowd was turning restive, beginning to feel those 'unpleasing sensations which arise from ungratified expectations'. Crosbie then chose a young acquaintance, a Trinity student named Richard McGwire, who weighed 114lbs or just over eight stone, to replace him. (The spelling of his name varies, but McGwire was the most common.) Some accounts say that McGwire volunteered from the crowd, while one says that he had already been invited to accompany Crosbie in the event of two people being able to travel. Crosbie had previously mentioned that he would take a companion on his second flight, so it is possible that they were friends. The whole affair was descending into farce when the highly agitated Crosbie again changed his mind, unwilling to yield all his great hopes to a substitute, and decided to make one further attempt on his own. McGwire gracefully withdrew. The *Dublin Journal* described the scene:

All the interior work of the boat was taken out, several feet of the balloon itself were cut off, all the ballast, his provisions and his last bottle of wine were thrown overboard and under all these disagreeable circumstances, Mr. Crosbie undauntedly determined to ascend. The gentlemen who held the boat pushed it upwards with all their strength but in vain; it rose a few feet from the impulse it had received but fell again, with no small degree of danger to Mr. Crosbie, at the other side of the square.

Crosbie finally accepted that he could not take off, and then, to add further to the confusion, another man (bizarrely, also named McGwire) rushed from the crowd and took his place in the basket, but he was prevailed upon to alight, while Richard McGwire resumed his place. Richard was given a quick lesson in balloon management, with the all-important valve cord being identified for him by somebody tying his ruffle to it. Eventually, the balloon rose with the twenty-year-old student on board, but not without alarming the crowd in the square when it came dangerously close to one of the Barracks chimneys. To the onlookers, it seemed that the balloon travelled opposite to the direction of the wind, seeming to confirm that there were upper currents of air different from those nearer land. McGwire was followed to the coast by balloon-chasers, young gentlemen on horseback, who watched him disappear over the sea. Among them were Lord Jocelyn, Lord Edward Fitzgerald, and Lord Henry Fitzgerald. Years later, Edward would earn an honoured place in Irish history as a leader of the United Irishmen. His horse went lame *en route* so he was not among a group who hired a boatman to continue the chase. The Duke of Rutland, who had been at the launch, took a keen interest in the safety of McGwire.

One observer, Ambrosia Lifford, wrote this accurate account of the flight to her brother in England:

Mr Crosbie has made the town wild. All this day he was to ascend with his balloon at twelve from the Barracks. I was quite satisfied with seeing him go up before from Ranelagh therefore I stayed quiet at home, but my daughters

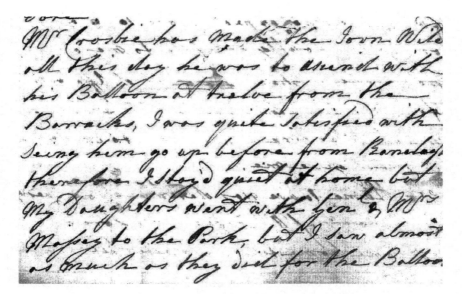

Extract from letter of Ambrosia Lifford. (Courtesy of Coventry Heritage and Arts Trust.)

went with Gen & Mrs. Massey to the Park, but I saw almost as much as they did for the balloon came over the Rotunda and Ballybough bridge, and I sat looking at it for an hour till it appeared no larger than a small ball. It was an uncommon clear day. Mr Crosbie did not go up with it for he was too heavy & it would not ascend with him but a Mr. McGwire a fine spirited young man of the College. It was thought he went out to sea, & there is now a report that the Balloon burst & he fell into the sea & was saved by a boat.

Her account was accurate. McGwire first attempted to land on Ireland's Eye but the valve cord had broken and he improvised by puncturing the balloon with a grappling hook. By that time he had drifted far from land and the damaged balloon had only two bags of ballast left, so McGwire chose discretion over valour, and came down at sea about nine miles east-north-east of Howth. The impact threw him out of the basket and his ankle became caught in a rope, so that he was ducked in the water several times before eventually freeing himself. Fortunately, he was an excellent swimmer, and he spent up to forty minutes in the water before being rescued by boatmen. Lord Henry Fitzgerald, Mr Thornton and Mr Oliver had paid boatmen five guineas to row them out and they soon arrived on the scene. The Duke and Duchess of Rutland waited patiently on shore to welcome the student aeronaut, and McGwire changed his clothes and took refreshments in a public house in Howth. Lord Henry collected about sixty guineas as a reward for the boatmen, and as an incentive to them to assist in future rescues.

McGwire received a hero's welcome in Dublin next day, and was chaired to Dublin Castle – to confer with the Viceroy and his wife – by fellow students in a procession led by a band. Rutland awarded him a knighthood and a commission in the army, he received a silver medal from Trinity College, and, of course, ballads were written about his exploit. The lionising he received from his fellow students was the most pleasing accolade to McGwire. These exceptional tributes for a last-minute substitute (who never made another flight) must have been galling to Crosbie, and one paper commented, 'We sympathise with Mr. Crosbie in his disappointment, as he nobly sacrificed his seat.' It must have been galling too to read this notice in the paper a few days later:

> Sir Richard McGwire begs leave to return his warmest thanks to the gentlemen of the college. The repetition of their kind attention marks a decided approbation, as much exceeding his merit as his powers of expression. Dr. Ussher begs leave to subjoin his particular thanks to those of his friend and pupil.

Crosbie's situation was compared to that of a gifted architect who was obliged to watch his creation being finished off by a workman, 'Though that workman might be applauded for executing the remaining part, yet it is not to the projector to whom the greater share is given.' One of the ballads written to celebrate McGwire began, 'Oh for a muse of fire/ That could ascend and emulate McGwire/ To sing

The preservation of Richard McGwire. Mezzotint by J.J. Barralet and W. Ward. The three men on the right are: Lord Henry Fitzgerald, Mr Oliver and Mr Thornton. (Courtesy of National Gallery of Ireland.)

his cool intrepid mind/ That dares adventurous to seek the skies/ That fearless braved the billows and the wind/ And stands a glorious object in a nation's eyes.'

It was noted that McGwire was not yet twenty-one years old and that he was only the second man ever to be knighted before he reached his majority. The other was Henry Plantagenet, who became King Henry V. Hodgson claimed that McGwire's exploit, 'though certainly exhibiting admirable pluck and spirit, was also characterized by an impulsive rashness which invited disaster'. The extreme risk of ballooning was highlighted one month later, when the tragic death of de Rozier, the first man to fly in a balloon, occurred over the English channel. This accident was a stark and shocking reminder of the extreme risks taken by the pioneers of flight.

Sir Richard
McGwire. (Courtesy
of the Board
of Trinity College
Dublin.)

Around this time too, public attitudes towards ballooning events were changing. The *Freeman's Journal* declared:

> While the brains of thousands seem turned into a sort of balloon madness, it is recommended of our industrious artizans to withdraw their views from the contemplation of the clouds, to that industrious utility which lies neglected at their feet. If the wealthy and scientific find an amusement in this new discovery they are not called upon by the cravings of want or the cries of family to repair the mischiefs of idleness. Those aerial experiments should be therefore removed to the Curragh of Kildare or some other interior parts where they cannot be productive of such general mischief as in the metropolis.

The Lord Mayor of Dublin, James Horan, was also alarmed at the number of people taking to the streets to watch balloon displays when they should be at work, and he banned them as a waste of people's time and 'very injurious to the public welfare'. It was hardly coincidence that the notice appeared in the press at the same time as reports of the Barracks flight, and while Potain's flight was imminent. France was declared to be on the point of banning, 'the pernicious custom of indiscriminate ballooning,' and especially Montgolfiere balloons – 'those destructive firebrands'. The town of Tullamore, Co. Offaly, was the scene of a disaster in May 1785, when a Montgolfiere balloon caused a fire which destroyed a hundred houses. The incident took place on a Fair Day and the balloon was released from Doctor Bleakley's yard by 'an English adventurer' encouraged by two gentlemen, for the amusement of their friends. It was blown against the chimney of the Barracks, first setting fire to Christopher Beck's house, and finally destroying all but five houses on Barrack Street. The distress and inconvenience was considerable, with scarcely enough accommodation left in the town to shelter those affected. A Mr Norris lost his house, offices and malthouse which contained a large amount of grain. Other similar accidents, on a smaller scale, were reported from around the country, and there was general condemnation of 'the absurd and dangerous practice' of releasing fire-balloons.

The *Dublin Journal* commended the Lord Mayor's ban, saying that, 'the liberating of lamp balloons was such a common practice that no less than twenty or thirty of them are let off almost every night to the great fear and terror of the inhabitants of this city'. In the countryside too there were dangers to hay and corn. The *Freeman's Journal* was convinced that the public had been sufficiently entertained by the balloons, and that, as it was, 'pretty certain that they can never be brought to be of any real utility, the magistrates or the legislature should interfere to prevent that great loss to the nation (never to be retrieved), the labour of our fellow citizens'. Clearly, the dream of a new golden age of flight was turning into a nightmare. There were, no doubt, many who would have shared the sentiments of this letter writer:

> The use of wings in any shape is not the gift of Providence to man; he
> should not therefore imitate what it will never be in his power to accom-
> plish – let him leave the feathered tribe in possession of their unrivalled
> prerogative.

A dissenting view came from a correspondent who urged that the ban
be dropped, and that the government should not only permit the sport
but patronise it, as a means of keeping the people happily occupied,
'Allow them only balloons and you need not dread Volunteers.'

The changed atmosphere towards ballooning is evident from a poem
published on 14 May. It was entitled 'To Richard Crosbie Esq. on his
attempting a Second Aerial Excursion, in which he proved unsuccessful'. It was written by an admirer of Richard Crosbie, but the references
to calumny, detraction and rancour capture the public animus towards
the hero of Ranelagh. The author was the poet and schoolmaster
Samuel Whyte, who ran a very successful academy in Grafton Street,
where Bewley's restaurant is now located and where a commemorative plaque can be seen. He had several famous students, among them
Richard Brinsley Sheridan, Robert Emmet, and Thomas Moore. His
methods were enlightened, and Moore later wrote appreciatively of his
'zeal and gentleness'. (In an introduction to a 1795 edition of Whyte's
poems, his son Edward claimed that he had been the very first to set off
a balloon in Ireland, as a boy in his father's school.)

> Tho' Envy, Crosbie, vilify thy name,
> And strive to blast the harvest of thy fame,
> 'Tis virtue's common lot; nor thou repine,
> The tribute due to great attempts is thine.
> Deep tho' the barbed shaft of Rancour pierce
> The sentence past, Time only can reverse.
> To Time, the impartial arbiter, submit,
> And let dark Calumny her venom spit.
> You, of Hibernia's sons, none can deny,

A Dedalus, first launched into the sky,
And with the flame of patriot glory fir'd,
To the third region of the air aspir'd.

Untutor'd and alone pursu'd your flight
Thro' untried space impervious to the sight.
So in the fiery car the Prophet caught,
Majestic rising pierc'd the azure vault,
Towards earth from high his awful presence bow'd
Look'd up and vanish'd thro' the impending cloud.

Eyes, take your last – thy soul's soft partner cried,
Her trembling infants clinging to her side,
While down her woe-wan cheeks the silent torrents glide.
What must the husband, what the father prove,
Leaving the weeping pledges of his love!
And, in his fate involv'd, where's the relief
To soothe the orphans' cries, the widow's grief?
Nature knock'd at his heart, but knock'd in vain,
His noble daring nothing can restrain;
Thro' Hope's perspective scenes remote he view'd,
Nor dreamt how near him dwelt ingratitude.
Generous as brave the Irish are renown'd,
In that presumption all his cares are drown'd,
And what his soul superior had conceiv'd,
He plann'd, constructed, gloriously achiev'd;
His country's fame among the nations rais'd,
Prov'd his desert and liberally was ---- prais'd.

But in the zenith of his triumph crost,
Chang'd is the scene, his occupation lost;
On frail foundations all his castles rear'd,
In one capricious moment disappear'd! –

The multitudes that gazed with straining eyes,
The tongues that rent with pealing shouts the skies,
The knees that suppliant for thy safety bent,
The astonish'd crowds that witnessed thy descent,
The hearts that ever with adoration glow'd,
The hands that flowers beneath thy footsteps strow'd,
Crosbie, more fickle than the inconstant wind,
Mere weathercocks to every gust you find;
And tho' exalted to the lunar sphere,
Foul mouthed detraction would pursue thee there;
The hard earned laurel from thy temples wrest,
And plant with thorns thy unoffending breast.
No wonder Babblers swell the daily lie,
When better judgments follow in the cry;
Injurious clamours raise on vague report,
And with the miseries of nature sport.
Lives there from human casualties exempt?
His crime imputed, What? His last attempt –
He fail'd – yet firmly to his purpose stood,
And all perform'd that art and nature could;
But still he fail'd – and nothing can atone
For disappointments – tho' the worst his own;
His fame, his fortune, what hadst thou at stake;
Blush, Censure, blush and retribution make.

Columbus thus his daring sails unfurl'd
Stemm'd seas unknown and gave another world
But found at last, to recompense his pains,
His throne a dungeon, and his trophies chains.

From wisdom merit consolation draws,
Not from the breath of popular applause.

Plaque
outside
Bewley's
of Grafton
Street.

Whyte's scathing comments on the unreliability of public acclaim and
the injustice to Crosbie are passionately felt. There are other references
to Crosbie in Samuel Whyte's collection of verse entitled *Poems on Various
Subjects* (1785), and the emptiness of public acclaim is again the theme:

> The topic now that every tongue engages
> The soil of past and theme of future ages
> Art's proudest boast and crown of speculation
> Is that phenomenon clep'd Aerostation.
> Each feeble amateur, believe his tale,
> Can ride the welkin and elude the gale;
> And like the finny tribes that range the ocean,
> Direct or retrograde, impel his motion.
> But why so long the experiment delay?
> Perhaps by compact Crosbie shown the way.

The enterprise proved him many a shout
But soon the storm of favour veered about.
He thought 'twould last! O, simple and absurd,
Even in the breath of praise he blame incurred.
Would it not make a very Stoic fret,
The world should benefits so soon forget?
Let them snarl on, or they with envy burst,
Tho' hardly treated, thou art not the first.
Scarcely an hour without example passes
Those who rely on public fame are asses.

It is interesting to note that Whyte was sensitive to the emotions felt by Crosbie's wife and family, as there are few references to them in newspaper sources. Crosbie's pursuit of his dream must have affected their lives in many ways, not least financially. Not only did he face the prospect of death each time he planned a flight, but his debts were guaranteed to mount each time also.

The whole issue of funding had dogged Crosbie since his first attempts. It was clear that there was a growing discontent among the public, notwithstanding the general acclaim for McGwire's flight. Harsh questions were being asked and the *Freeman's Journal* rejected one ballad about Crosbie on the grounds that it was 'too sarcastic and, in our opinion, unmerited'. In the *Dublin Journal* of 21 May 1785, Crosbie addressed these issues when he asked citizens for 'a suspension of their censure' until he had a further chance to prove himself. He explained that he had lost a large amount of money at the two Royal Barracks events, and that while gate receipts amounted to £393, this covered little more than half the expense. He announced that he was engaged in drawing up a statement of all his receipts and expenses since he first began his experiments in Ranelagh and would present it to the public. It seems that he was adopting a policy of full accountability with regard to money, to counter rumours that he was making a fortune. (Crosbie was not alone in his financial woes: by this time, Hollister was intent on selling Ranelagh Gardens after 'a long course of unremitted annual loss'.)

Crosbie's committee inspected his accounts and informed the public that he was certainly out of pocket after all his experiments, to the amount of £447 4s 9½d. This amount would have the spending worth of approximately €32,000 today. The committee consisted of the Earl of Charlemont (chairman), the Earl of Roden, Col. French, R.H. Hutchinson, John La Touche, Esq., Sir Richard McGwire, Sir Frederick Flood, Counsellor Whitestone, Revd Mr Austin and Dr Aikin. R. Cuthbert was secretary, and Mr Cunliffe took the money at the Barracks gate. One notable former supporter, Dr Ussher, was not listed, but it is interesting that McGwire was involved, since he certainly owed his fame and status entirely to Crosbie. The committee also exonerated Crosbie from any 'want of judgment or attention' during the Barracks events. In June, the committee met in the King's Arms, Smock Alley, and approved of Crosbie's new balloon, significantly noting that it was 'adapted to his own weight'.

Crosbie announced that his next plan was to take off from the Fifteen Acres in the Phoenix Park, and to have the event open to the public at no charge. The balloon was to be 'proportionate to his weight' and the announcement was expressly an attempt 'to re-instate himself in public favour, which misfortune not his fault unhappily deprived him of,' after the Barracks debacle. His next flight did take place in July 1785, but he took off not from the Fifteen Acres, but from the more august surroundings of Leinster House, home of the Duke of Leinster.

The *Volunteer Evening Post* was one of the papers which berated Crosbie for wasting people's time and causing idleness and dissipation. However, it also acknowledged that ballooning had provided useful information on the nature and properties of air and on wind currents. The writer also speculated that balloons could be useful in exploring inaccessible mountains, in war, in reconnaissance, in sending express communications and communicating with places under siege. But the author also seemed to have a distinct sense of the symbolic magnificence of ballooning, the entertainment it provided and the transcendence that it offered:

> At any rate, conceived of as an entertainment, they certainly furnish the most magnificent and sublime that men were ever spectators of. They give us the right of dominion as it were, over other elements, and realise to us in some degree that fancied communication between earth and the celestial worlds, in which the enthusiasm of ancient poetry so much delighted.

Among the many poems written about ballooning these are some more of dubious merit but with insights into how the public saw the whole spectacle. These lines are from the *Dublin Evening Post*, June 1785:

> Nought but balloons will now go down
> In Dublin and in Edgeworthstown.
> Balloons the talk from morn to noon –
> Perhaps they first came from the moon;
> For lunacy I do suspect
> Ballooners often does infect.
> Go where you will, or out or in,
> A beau you'll meet with a balloon pin,
> Balloon buckles and balloon brooch,
> And some must have their balloon coach.
> And since the balloon's so much the fashion,
> For which some have the strongest passion,
> Oh let us see then, if we can,
> Of what great use they are to man.
> Of great use they are in war:
> Intelligence may bring from far:
> And did you want a siege to raise,
> You soon may send in what you please.
> Beseiged long cannot want relief –
> Balloons can carry bread or beef.
> But did you want a town to burn,

Balloons may serve for that same turn,
For proof of which word say no more,
Referring here to Tullamore.

These lines were written by 'Pillon':

Ye high and low fliers of all ranks attend
And counsel receive from an aeronaut friend.
Your coaches and chariots henceforth lay aside –
Prepare in balloons thro' the skies all to ride;
With dust of vile roads who'd be choked or be blind,
Like witches on brooms you may post on the wind.
O'er valleys, high hills and wide seas you may sweep,
And into the moon your own sphere take a peep.

7

FROM LEINSTER LAWN
INTO THE IRISH SEA

Mortification after mortification!

Richard Crosbie

Richard Crosbie made one last ascent in Dublin, on 19 July 1785, from Leinster Lawn rather than the Fifteen Acres. Papers were very confident that this time he would succeed, 'This enterprising aeronaut will not rest till he has accomplished his bold and noble undertaking'. The silk for the envelope was manufactured by Mr Williams of Francis Street, whose efficiency helped Crosbie to expedite his plans. (Watson's *Almanack and Directory* of 1786 lists Henry Williams of 26 Francis Street as a silk manufacturer.) The Duke of Leinster was praised for providing the venue while the Lord Mayor was trying to implement his ban; he was described as a, 'steady patriot, great man, discoverer and cherisher of real talent'. Of the many newspaper accounts of the event, the most authoritative appeared in Faulkner's *Dublin Journal,* with this covering letter to Mr Faulkner:

Sir,

As a circumstantial account of my last aerial voyage on Tuesday the 19th instant may prove agreeable to my generous countrymen, I think it a duty incumbent on me as far as possible, to gratify their curiosity; and I trust it will not be thought too long by the Printer of a Paper who seems to have in view the same object in all his publications.

I am, Sir,

Your humble servant,

Richard Crosbie.

There was such a demand for copies of the *Dublin Journal* with Crosbie's account that it was reprinted several times, to the delight of Mr Thomas Todd Faulkner of Parliament Street, no doubt. Crosbie began by describing the unfavourable weather at 5a.m. which convinced members of his committee that it was too risky to attempt a flight; heavy squalls continued and at 8a.m. they confirmed this decision. By then, large numbers of people had gathered outside Leinster House, on the Merrion Square side, and they were showing signs of restlessness. Crosbie then decided to bring the balloon out to see if it might be possible to go ahead with the plan. At about 10a.m., 'some officious person' fired a gun in town and this led to general firing, the usual signal to announce an ascent; this convinced Crosbie that he had to proceed. His boat or gondola had a number of bladders attached to it, to aid in flotation, and he also carried a cork jacket for emergencies. At about 2.20p.m., the Duchess of Rutland cut the rope, releasing the balloon.

His ascent was difficult, as some friends were holding the basket down while others were trying to push it up, and his carriage struck the ha-ha wall which enclosed Leinster Lawn. With some assistance and by dropping some ballast, he managed to rise, but again struck the ground in fields opposite Merrion Square. He did succeed in ascending, with 50lbs of his ballast of 300lbs already thrown out, and 'above 60,000 spectators were divided in admiration between the beautiful form and colour of the balloon and barge, the majesty of their progress, the cheerfulness and collected management of Mr. Crosbie, and the sublimity of the whole'. After thirty-two minutes Crosbie disappeared from view and the agreed signal of a volley of shots was fired by the Volunteers. Crosbie was probably unaware of an incident at the launch in which several people were injured when a crush caused the collapse of a wall. Most of the injuries were minor cuts and bruises, with one woman named Elizabeth Dillon suffering a broken arm. Barrington, with typical hyperbole, claims that several people died, but this was not reported in any newspaper accounts.

Newspapers were fully confident that this sea crossing would be successful. The *Volunteer Evening Post* went to press convinced that Crosbie's 'character as an intrepid and able aeronaut [was] now fully established.' Verses headed 'Lines on Mr. Crosbie's ascencion' once again hailed his exploits:

Crosbie's ascent from Leinster Lawn. (Courtesy of National Library of Ireland.)

Yes, Crosbie, Heaven directed, go!
Nor longer with impatience burn.
The rage of envy overthrow
And millions hail thy quick return.
Thrice happy spot whence treasured lore
Thus beams its bright, its genuine dawn
Till Time shall wing his flight no more,
Fame fix thy seat in Leinster Lawn.

The next edition, however, had a prose column headed 'Mr. Crosbie's descension'. His direction at first was thought to be towards Whitehaven. Crosbie soon relished his freedom and his unprecedented bird's-eye view of Dublin and the coast:

I now took a view of the astonishing scene I was quitting, and after returning the salutations of the innumerable spectators along the fields, Strand &c to the seashore, I was highly entertained with a race composed of hundreds of horsemen, stretching with full speed along the Pigeon House Wall, as if their course could not be terminated. I was now over the bay and as I imagined from the diminution of objects that I was still ascending, I cast my eye on the barometer, which to my mortification I found had lost a considerable quantity of Mercury from the two concussions I had received against the wall and ground on my ascent …

I marked the height of the mercury with my pencil, and some time after, one of the bladders that was in the carriage with me bursting with a considerable explosion, I looked to the barometer and found it had fallen a few inches. I marked the fall and for a considerable period seemed to move in a favourable direction. I took out my pen, ink and paper to write down such observations as I could make, and to entrust to a faithful record those thoughts which the glorious and unbounded scene around me inspired me with.

I had written about a page when I felt myself grow very chilly, and put on an oiled silk wrapper, which soon brought on a glow of heat. I had two thermometers, one with Mercury and the other with spirits of wine, both had at this time fallen so low that the Mercury and spirits had entirely descended into their respective bulbs. My ink was so frozen that I could not use it, until holding the bottle some time in my hand, its contents again became fluid. I at this time perceived the great advantage of my lower valve, for perceiving the smell of the gaz, I was for a moment roused from the subject which I was then committing to paper, and looking up to the balloon, observed the valve open at short intervals with a sort of pulsation, and at each discharging the inflammable air in considerable quantities. The balloon was expanded to its fullest extent, and a number of bladders that were attached to my carriage exploded one after another in some measure resembling hedge-firing.

Tho' the height was now so considerable that every cloud in the atmo-sphere was far below me, and nothing above but a blue expanse, I felt no sort of inconvenience or difficulty in breathing, but taking an observation from a line which the Light-house wall formed, tho' indistinct, and the Wicklow shore, which had appeared to my view beyond Bray-head, I found that I was stationary or nearly so, what little way I was making being to the Southward; I was nevertheless so charmed with the enchanting scene below me, that for a while I forgot my enterprise, but the appearance of the British shore soon recalled me to myself, and observing the wreck flying to Eastward, as it seemed over the surface of the water, I opened my lower valve only, both to assist the efforts of the superabundant or compressed air to release itself and to descend into the favourable current; in this I suc-ceeded and as yet had not parted with any ballast from the time of my ascent, tho' nearly half channel over. I attentively watched the rise of the mercury and observing it to arrive at the mark I had before made, when in the same stratum of clouds, I was in hopes it would stop there, but rising still higher, and the balloon consequently descending, I threw out four pounds of sand, when the mercury became settled and afterwards gradually rose to about the mark I mention. I now moved forward with considerable velocity, as I could perceive from passing some vessels that were holding the same course. I encountered a light shower of hail, and flying in all directions which however soon passed off. Some humid vapour that had ascended with the gaz into the balloon in the inflation, fell in large drops from the bottom, which wetted my paper and blotted my notes while I marked them down, I attentively watched my timekeeper that I had laid on a bag of ballast, in the bottom of my carriage. My course now bid so fair for success that I experienced more happiness and transport in the idea than I believe ever before fell to the lot of man. My mind that was hitherto voluptuously fed, made me inattentive to the cravings of my appetite, which at length grew rather pressing, and with my pen in one hand and part of a fowl in the other, I wrote as I enjoyed my delicious repast.

In this account he gives some specific details of his note-taking and his observations, perhaps to highlight the scientific as distinct from the entertainment aspect of the voyage. Back in Dublin, first reports were equally confident that Crosbie would make the British shore by 6p.m. He observed a shower of hail, which passed over without too much effect, and he continued as before. He had a distinct view of the shores of Ireland and England, and, in other accounts, he was reported as saying that, 'it was impossible to give the human imagination any adequate idea of the unspeakable beauties which the scenery of the sea bounded by both lands presented. It was such as would make me risk a life to enjoy again'. Although he does not mention it in his own account, he was reported as suffering 'a strong propulsion on the tympanum of the ears' and a sickness caused by the anxiety and fatigue of the day. He was drawing a sketch of the scene when he heard a gunshot down below and saw that a sailboat was following the same course as he was. He responded with a shout and a wave of his flag, and was surprised that he could hardly hear his own voice, and had pain in both ears. The boat was the Dunleary barge under Captain Walnutt, which was providing an escort for him courtesy of the authorities.

Weather conditions now caused havoc with the flight. Another shower of hail came on, accompanied by violent squalls, and he realised that he was losing height again. He threw out some ballast but found that it had no effect and he was powerless to prevent his fall into the sea. He was not despairing however, 'I was convinced that I could ascend again, from the peculiar construction of my carriage, when the shower was over, therefore was but a little alarmed, as only my legs were wet'. Water entered the boat and acted as a form of ballast in fact. Unfortunately the valve was releasing hydrogen and the lifting power was not adequate. He dropped the chain over the side to see if that would allow him to rise, but this gave him no advantage. He proceeded to don the cork jacket which he had almost forgotten about, ready for a ducking. The wind continued to drive the balloon along:

> I therefore, though with undescribable mortification at not being able to
> fly, reconciled myself to the idea of being ignominiously towed to the other
> side, as I was drifting through the water with astonishing celerity. However,
> looking behind me, I observed a vessel crowding sail after me, but as I
> watched her a good while, I perceived she was losing way.

It seems that the balloon acted as a sail, driving Crosbie along faster than the boat. Captain Walnutt eventually caught up with him, and at 3.47p.m., Crosbie was rescued after spending twenty-six minutes in the water. He managed to save the balloon and bring it on deck. One of the sailors, who was holding a rope attached to the balloon, went frantic when he was lifted clear off the boat as the balloon rose in a gust; fortunately he was hauled back to safety. The boat arrived back in Dún Laoghaire at 4a.m., having been becalmed for some hours. 'The mortification I felt at not accomplishing my intended voyage,' wrote Crosbie, 'was greatly mitigated by the almost undoubted certainty and safety, which, I have every reason to conceive, there is in crossing the channel, on any particular occasion, with a proper wind and in good weather.' Ever optimistic and forward-looking, he was not overwhelmed by disappointment, firmly believing that he would in due time achieve his aim. Crosbie says that he was ten leagues from Howth when rescued, other accounts say fourteen leagues. A league was approximately three miles. He lost the notes he had made, and his watch, which he specifically states was his own construction and work, was ruined.

also the laſt; and it was very improper that ſuch a ſpurious petition ſhould be brought in, as even the chairman of the meeting had not ſigned it.

It was therefore withdrawn at the deſire of Mr. Ward; after which the Houſe adjourned to this day.

Mr. Croſbie's Balloon.

Yeſterday morning, about eleven o'clock, Mr. Croſbie gave notice to the public of his intention of taking his aerial voyage, by beating of drums, &c. the moment it was known, the front of the lawn before the Duke of Leinſter's houſe, began to be crouded, and every other place where there was a poſſibility of ſeeing the Balloon. At about half paſt two o'clock the public expectation, and the wiſhes of his numerous friends were highly gratified, and his character as an intrepid and able aeronant fully eſtabliſhed, by the Balloon being liberated amid the acclamations of thouſands of his applauding countrymen; his ſpirited perſeverance in ſtruggling through many difficulties marks his character for undaunted reſolution and wiſdom. The moment the Balloon was liberated it ſkimmed along the ground of the lawn, and ſlightly touched the parapet wall in Merrion-ſtreet, but without any other injury than his being thrown on one ſide of the netting; he then with utmoſt preſence of mind threw out ſome ſand with his hands on which the Balloon gently roſe, but proceeding heavily he diſcharged two bags of ballaſt, on which it aſcended in the moſt majeſtic manner, taking its direction over the heads of the admiring multitude, through the middle of the Square towards Ringſend, and apparently proceeded in a Weſt South Weſt direction till at length he was enveloped in a dark cloud. The current of air above blew in a ſimilar direction to that below; and there

Theatre-Royal, Smock-alley.

This Evening, will be preſented the Tragedy of
MACBETH.
Macbeth, Mr. Henderſon, Lady Macbeth, Mrs. Barnes.
To which will be added,
BARNABY BRITTLE.
Mr. Brittle, Mr. Moſs, Mrs. Brittle Miſs Jarrat.

To-morrow Evening,
The FAIR PENITENT.
Sciolto, Mr. Aickin, Lothario, Mr. Holman, and Horatio, Mr. Pope.

Mr. DALY's BENEFIT.
On Thurſday the 28th inſtant, a new Tragedy, never acted here, called,
The Myſterious Huſband

Lord Davenant, Mr. Henderſon, Captain Dormer, Mr. Pope, Sir Harry Barlow, Mr. Aickin, Sir Edmund Travers, Mr. Moſs, Paget, Mr. Hurſt, and Charles Davenant, Mr. Holman.
Marianne, Mrs. Barnes, Writing Woman, Mrs. O'Neill, and Lady Davenant, Miſs Younge.
To which will be added the Maſque of
COMUS.
Comus, Mr. Henderſon, and Principal Bacchanal, Mr. Johnſtone.
Places in the Boxes to be taken of Mr. Marſh at the Box-Room.

Freeman's Journal report of Leinster Lawn flight. (Courtesy of National Library of Ireland.)

He returned to a great welcome in Dublin, and his flight received much publicity, with paintings and engravings celebrating the event. Other newspaper accounts carry further details of his reception. He was invited to breakfast with the Duke and Duchess of Rutland, who were staying at their summer residence, Mr Lees' elegant lodge, Blackrock House. He was later escorted into town by Lord Ranelagh and Sir Frederick Flood, chairman of his committee. He visited the Duke of Leinster and the provost of Trinity, John Hely-Hutchinson, before being carried shoulder high, first to Dublin Castle and finally to his home in Cumberland Street, 'amidst the acclamation of surrounding thousands'. In a private letter, however, which found its way to the *Dublin Evening Post*, Crosbie revealed his true feelings, and once again his emotional state is that of mortification:

> Mortification after mortification! At half channel over, at about a quarter after three o'clock, an unfortunate squall of wind precipitated me into the seas in spite of every effort to prevent it by throwing out a large quantity of ballast, but just as I seemed to overcome the impetus of the descent, the machine took the water and was thereby prevented from rising again. I was towed nearly a league, though in perfect safety, and indeed ease, until I was overtaken and received on board by Dunleary barge, commanded by Captain Walnutt.

Crosbie was duly honoured with a tribute performance of Richard Brinsley Sheridan's play *The Rivals*, which was staged by the Benevolent Theatre Society (of which Crosbie was a member) in the Theatre Royal, Smock Alley in late July. It was a fundraising event to help him with his plans for another flight. As was customary, a special epilogue was written for the occasion and was delivered by the leading actress, Miss Younge. The audience responded with 'the loudest and most deserved plaudits':

> They'll say perhaps that we've played a foolish part
> Thus to encourage the ballooning art!

A bold attempt don't make the merit less
- 'Tis not in mortals to command success.'
And sure your candour will this hope retain,
Tho' it failed once, it may not fail again.

The time may come, perhaps it now approaches,
When we may use balloons like ships and coaches,
Travel through nations which the sky enshrouds
And sail for future commerce in the clouds.
See our young bucks, whose gigs so high and fleet
Now reach the upper regions – of the street;
Whose heads have long been rambling in the moon.
Cry – 'Tie on my car there – give me my balloon,
Last night's debauch has made me cursed dry,
I'll take some ice and cool me in the sky.'

Ye Sunday cits go leave your cars and noddies,
And now ascend in state like Gods and Goddesses,
Yourselves to heaven, and your amusements trust,
And take the air without a dread of dust,
The dying nymph and her romantic swain,
May quit the earth and all its prying train;
Mount in the chariot that balloons have given,
To find if marriages are made in Heaven.
For new intrigues – Oh, what a charming hope!
Amidst the clouds to love – and then elope –
Thus if balloons to science are no use,
These good effects they may at least produce.

Thus to encourage and improve the plan,
Let us unite and aid it all we can,
Through your protection CROSBIE'S fame shall rise,
And public favour – lift him to the skies.

In October 1785, Crosbie announced his intention of making another attempt, but by then public interest was clearly on the wane. The announcement in the press stated that tickets would cost 3*s* 3*d* and could be booked in advance, but the actual date and time would be not be made known until nearer the launch. There would be no public signals, but subscribers would receive the details by special delivery well in advance. The press notice appeared throughout November, with a final statement that subscriptions would close on the 23 November. 'If there is not an adequate sum subscribed, as he has already been so very considerable a loser, Mr. Crosbie must, though with the utmost reluctance, relinquish his design for the present.' He promised that, in that event, all money already subscribed would be returned.

There are no further reports of this attempt, and it must be assumed that it never took place. Crosbie never did achieve his goal of crossing the Irish Sea, which was finally accomplished thirty-two years later, in 1817, by the son of James Sadler. Nevertheless, he was undaunted and had one more balloon adventure in Ireland, when he did fly across a channel, albeit no wider than the Shannon estuary.

Leinster Lawn today.

8

SOARING OVER THE SHANNON: CROSBIE'S FINAL FLIGHT

The true Columbus of the trackless air.

Ballad

Richard Crosbie's final flight in Ireland took place in April 1786, and it was a successful but expensive adventure. The *Freeman's Journal* of 8-11 April declared that Crosbie's intention was to make a flight from Limerick to Cork and then to proceed to Dublin. The paper wished him well, recalling that he had given great pleasure and entertainment to the people of Dublin on many occasions. It noted that ballooning events were a greater novelty outside of Dublin, so Crosbie's plan to go to the provinces did make sense. It certainly was true that people all over Europe who had not themselves witnessed a balloon ascending were inclined to disbelieve the stories they heard about such events. Moving outside Dublin must have made sense to Crosbie, as there was obviously balloon-fatigue in the capital by 1786, and more eager audiences and sponsors elsewhere, perhaps.

From December 1785 onwards, details of the slow progress of Crosbie's plans for an aerial voyage were reported in the *Limerick*

Chronicle, and summarised by Larry Walsh in the *Old Limerick Journal* (Winter 1994). Crosbie began by displaying his 'Hibernian Balloon' in the Assembly Room, at a price of 1s 1d, from 10a.m. to 4p.m. each day. This price was fixed by Crosbie himself to make the event affordable to as many as possible, and it is again an indication that he was managing the business aspect of the event. The public was assured that 'good fires will be continually kept' and miniature balloons were also sent up for their entertainment. A meeting of prominent Limerick people was held, with Edmond Henry Pery in the chair. A committee of nine men was set up to gather subscriptions; these were George Smyth, Capt. Petries, Revd Dean Crosbie, Doctor Maunsell, Philip Roche, Richard Harte, Charles Sargent, Henry Fosbery and John Howley. Other prominent figures gave their support afterwards, for example, Sir Richard de Burgho, Sir Henry Hartstonge, Sir Vere Hunt, Hon. Silver Oliver, John Tuthill, Thomas Jackson, Edward Moore, Augustine Fitzgerald, Walter Widenham, George Maunsell, Revd John Quin and Standish Grady.

The House of Industry today.

The flight was first planned for 2 January 1786, but it was to take several more months before preparations were completed. The House of Industry (the Poorhouse) on the North Strand (now Clancy Strand) was offered as the location. One guinea was set as the minimum subscription, and this covered seven tickets to the launch, with non-subscribers to pay 4s 4d on the day. Crosbie had to return to Dublin to obtain sulphuric acid and the iron filings needed to generate hydrogen, confirming that much of the procuring of the materials fell to him. By early March, subscriptions were only trickling in and the paper admonished all the collectors to be more active:

> Travelling in the air is an improvement in science which has excited the admiration of all Europe; scarce a town in Scotland but enabled Mr. Lunardi to gratify their curiosity by generous subscription and donations. It is indeed a spectacle grand and beautiful beyond description, and it will reflect great credit on the taste of the inhabitants of Limerick to encourage Mr. Crosbie in his exertions for their entertainment.

Colonel Prendergast Smyth and William Causabon Harrison were added to the committee, specifically to ensure that more people subscribed. There was something of a public outcry against the committee for not exerting themselves more energetically in raising funds, and the *Chronicle* railed that while there would be no difficulty in raising funds for a horse race or a cock fight, science and art were despised, 'and the most delightful of all exhibitions which would enlighten the understandings and charm the eyes of the learned as well as the illiterate is trampled on and neglected'. By early April only a quarter of the amount needed had been collected, but nevertheless, the flight was fixed for the 26 April at 2p.m., weather permitting. Crosbie must have improved his method of inflating the balloon by this time because he allowed just two hours, from 12a.m. to 2p.m., for the process. Traffic plans were once again enforced: people were encouraged to come early and carriages coming over Thomond Bridge would have to remain on the Strand beyond the House of Industry until proceedings were over, so that they did not cause an obstruction. Several gentlemen on good horses would be standing by to follow the course of the balloon.

Yet once more, problems arose to prevent the flight on 26 April: the casks were not strong enough to hold the sulphuric acid and Crosbie was obliged to postpone the flight until the following day, and to ask for people's forgiveness. 'Every man of humanity, every lady of sensibility felt for his situation, and they bore the disappointment with not the least marks of anger.' In fact, it was admirable caution that made Crosbie wait; far too often in flights everywhere, pressure from the public and fear of disappointing them made the first airmen take risks. The launch went ahead at about 4.30p.m. on Thursday 27 April before a crowd estimated variously at 50,000 and 60,000. Crosbie's coolness, prudence, intrepidity and genius were admired. He wore a crimson jacket and white breeches. Those assisting were Dean Crosbie, Sir Vere Hunt, Sir Richard de Burgho, Colonel Smyth, Colonel Knight, and Colonel Harte. There were many foreigners present and 'it was universally agreed that his ascent was a noble one, and the best ever made in Europe'. The balloon was visible over Limerick city for an hour and twenty minutes and then drifted westwards along the Shannon towards Tarbert.

Crosbie's own account was published in the *Chronicle* of 1 May and it is an invaluable source of information:

> After so many and such very flattering testimonies of approbation which I have met with in this city, I should think myself wanting in duty and gratitude if I omitted any relation that might communicate amusement or gratify a laudable curiosity ...
>
> The happy moment at length arrived which put me in sole possession of all that could charm the eye of man and gratify my warmest ambition. As I gradually ascended, the expanding landscape presented such a scene as no pen can describe; the river Shannon with all its little islands formed a pleasing variety I had before been unacquainted with. I determined to make a

Crosbie's balloon over Limerick, on the left. *History of Limerick* by John Ferrar. (Courtesy of National Library of Ireland.)

drawing of it, and had scarcely ended my salutations to the fair assemblage I had left, now become undistinguishable, when I assumed my paper and pencil and began to chart, but when I reached a considerable altitude, I found my drawing had been false, as I commenced it on an extended scale that was diminishing as I ascended. I now examined my barometer which had stood at 30 [inches] on earth and found it had fallen to 15 [inches]. I hung out my grappling in order to clear the rope to which it was fastened, and that it should act as a plummet, by which means I could accurately perceive the course I took, and as I was exceedingly tossed about by the agitation of the atmosphere in the ascent, I concluded there prevailed several different currents, which I at once determined to explore, and the experiment in the end gave me exquisite delight.

I observed the course I was now taking was almost due west, exactly over the Shannon and could perceive a rapid approach towards the Western Ocean. I made a note of the degree at which my barometer stood, 15, and ascended till it fell to 13, where I got a current from NNE, by which I was conveyed over Tarbert and part of the county of Kerry. I was anxious to see the mountains of Kerry, but could perceive nothing more in appearance than a figured plain chequered like a carpet. The prospect was unbounded but by accumulating clouds which formed my horizon, I could plainly see the Lake of Killarney, but those sonorous hills which surround it were leveled with the surface.

He believed that he was stationary and he took the opportunity to eat some food, and drink a bottle of wine to the health of his friends on earth:

> I had been obliged before to put on my oil silk wrapper, and now experienced its utility; my feet and hands however were very cold and as I was determined to explore a higher region, I had recourse to a phial of strong lavender drops to keep warm, which I drank off without observing the strength of them, as every humid thing about me had been frozen, the lavender drops and the bottle they were in felt as warm as if they had been at the fire.

Crosbie then says that he ascended to a higher altitude than he had ever done before; he took barometer readings as he progressed, and at his highest point it read ten inches. He experienced great difficulty in breathing and acute pain in his ears:

> The difficulty of breathing I had before experienced was now increased to a considerable degree, my heart beat with astonishing rapidity, and my ears, from the dilation of the cellular vessels, felt as if going to burst. My breath congealing on the instant of respiration fell like a light snow, and collected on my lap as it dropped. As I had not taken any additional covering but my loose gown, my feet and hands became intensely cold and my fingers cramped, but to my astonishment, the difficulty in breathing gradually decreased, and the pain in my ears became less; these circumstances, adding to my having got into a current which carried me eastward, and in a right direction for Limerick again, determined me to stay in the same altitude until I had got nearly over the city.

It is notable that while Crosbie's account gives details of his barometer readings, and he mentions that he reached 'a considerable altitude', he never specifies a particular height. In response to the newspaper's claim that he was three and a quarter miles high, a correspondent wrote to the *Freeman's Journal* that that must a great exaggeration, 'as a human being could not possibly breathe' at that height.

He continued his readings and exploration of the effects of the currents until nearly 6p.m. The River Shannon appeared 'like a white silk thread in a green piece of cloth'. He expected to land near Limerick city, but the balloon was carried over Clare towards Dromoland Castle, seat of Sir Lucius O'Brien. Observing its cultivated grounds, Crosbie was determined to descend there. The open space within the estate would have made the landing safer, but he was carried past it and landed in a nearby field, in the townland of Ballygireen near Newmarket-on-Fergus. Securing the balloon to a stone wall he began to take out his equipment, calling for help from some of the people who had begun to gather. But 'to my great mortification ... astonishment and fear lent them wings and they fled from me with precipitation'. He managed to hold the balloon by himself as he tried to fill it with stones from the wall, but found himself being dragged along by it towards the River Fergus, and eventually had to let it go and suffer 'the mortification to see my chariot re-ascend without me'. The owner of the land, Mr Singleton, sent help and Crosbie spent the night in his house. He also visited Dromoland the following day. The balloon eventually came to rest near Ennis and was recovered by Captain O'Brien, but was too badly damaged to be usable.

When news of the empty basket reached Limerick, it was feared at first that Crosbie was dead and there was great relief when he returned to Limerick on the evening after his flight. He arrived at 9p.m. and was hailed by the populace. The horses were removed from his carriage, which was then drawn by the people. 'There were illuminations, bonfires and every demonstration of joy which a grateful people could show to their honoured and distinguished countryman'. On the following day he was again chaired through the city, all the trades presented him with cockades for his hat, and ships' masters were particularly appreciative. A 'handsome sum' was collected for Crosbie. The band of the 21st Regiment played 'The Conquering Hero' for him, and one writer hoped that, 'the friends of genius and lovers of science would at some future period erect an obelisk on North Strand, where he ascended'. People who had seen Lunardi, de Rozier and Blanchard ascend declared that none had done so with the same *éclat* as Crosbie.

Crosbie was to receive the freedom of the city in a valuable gold box, and there was a report of a subscription being raised for a second flight from Limerick to Cork, but nothing seems to have come of this. The *Volunteer Journal* had speculated that Crosbie's Limerick flight might end in Dublin, and it also claimed that Crosbie was invited to Kerry to launch a flight from either Tralee or Killarney. This would have brought him very close to Ardfert, the place where his ancestor Bishop John Crosbie had first established the line.

Limerick celebrated for three days and ballads were again composed about the event:

> Hail gen'rous Crosbie, whose exploits will crown
> Thy native land with honour and renown.
> Words cannot paint what Crosbie dares to view
> One vast expanse of universal blue.
> Where yon bright orb, th'eternal source is found
> Of light and life to every world around;
> The glorious prospect animates his soul
> While clouds and vapours far beneath him roll.
> Ne'er will his countrymen forget his name
> While distant nations will resound his fame.
>
> CROSBIE, all hail! whose strong enlightened mind,
> With love of science and with sense refined,
> Through realms of ether, who could boldly soar,
> Unbounded earth to view and Heaven to explore.

Tho' cloud capt towers shall moulder into dust
And all the conquerors trophies turn to rust
Yet Crosbie's name to future time shall live
And to Hibernia lasting Honour give.

The *Chronicle* was particularly impressed by the insouciance displayed by Crosbie as he enjoyed a drink in the sky:

To lose sight of the terrestrial globe and to be wrapt up in the clouds must produce sensations which are beyond our conception; but to quaff the wine to his friends below when he was three miles above them, when he had clouds for his footstool and the azure heavens for his canopy, was a banquet which the gods themselves must have smiled on with approbation. After gratifying us sublunary mortals with a sight so magnificent, awful and delighting, after travelling so far on the tender sighs of as many earthly goddesses as were ever seen in one group – it is no wonder that Mr. Crosbie should be received by the grateful people of Limerick with distinguished honours.

The *Chronicle* published a long poem called *The Aeronaut*, which began by ranking Crosbie among the eminent scientists of all time. The poem gave a survey of his life from his early childhood, accurately alluding to some of his early experiences.

Those rare endowments, restless, uncontroll'd
Kind nature mix'd in Crosbie's happy mould.
Eccentric, studious, enterprising, wild,
Fair Science mark'd him for her fav'rite child.

Monastic strictures check'd his soaring mind,
Quaint, common rules uncommon parts confin'd.
At length in slow succession came the hour,
For latent genius to display its pow'r.

This tow'ring youth no distant mears could bound
His mind took in the vast creation's round.
Both seas and earth already known, the skies
Were th'only field for future enterprise.

The poem refers to his difficulties in college, and the support he received from the Viceroy:

His airy scheme the Fellows disapprove
No new essays the silent Sister move.
A royal patron lent his ready aid
Their trials furnished and their labours paid.

The poem ends by declaring that Crosbie would forever rank among the great aeronauts:

On their records fam'd Crosbie will appear,
The true Columbus of the trackless air.
Kings, viceroys and the pension'd things they've made
Will crouch despis'd in blank oblivion's shade,
When Crosbie's boundless philosophic rage
Shall shine in th'epic or historic page.

After the celebrations, Crosbie called a meeting of the committee, anxious to settle his accounts and return to Dublin. A list of approximately 130 subscribers was published on 11 May, and it showed that the largest subscription was £10 from Sir Vere Hunt. John P. Smyth gave £8, Edmond Henry Pery £5, Sir Richard de Burgho, Standish Grady and Richard Harte £4 each, while most on the list gave £1. The totals were as follows:

Amount raised in subscriptions: £213 17s 0d
Amount taken at gate: £29 0s 8d

Total Expenses: £415 7s 9d
Loss to Mr Crosbie: £172 10s 1d

This loss amounted to approximately €12,000 in today's terms. Crosbie must by now have been in considerable financial difficulty. Even if he appeared carefree in the air over the Shannon, he must have had deep anxieties about his future and about the debts he had acquired from pursuing his dream. It is ironic in the light of Crosbie's financial worries that his sister, a Mrs Douglas, inherited a large amount of money in 1787. A wealthy Irishman in London left 'most of his plentiful fortune' to her in acknowledgement of support he received as a young man from her father, Sir Paul, when they were in the same regiment. What a difference this bequest might have made if Richard had been the beneficiary.

Perhaps buoyed up by his success in Limerick, Crosbie made one final attempt to organise a flight in the summer of 1786, and Belfast was his intended location. He first approached Lord Charlemont seeking assistance and the earl wrote immediately to his friend Dr Alexander Haliday in Belfast on 29 May:

> Here has been just now my friend, the aerial Crosbie, who having some idea of carrying his balloon to Belfast, in order that it may from thence carry him across the Channel, swears to me that he cannot think of going thither without having the honour and pleasure of being known to Doctor Haliday. The man is perfectly right and I have not a word to offer in contradiction to his wise resolution, and so I am obliged to sit down and beg of you to suffer him to wait on you at his arrival … I will make no apologies; indeed, in the present instance, I need them less than I usually do, as your trouble will be paid by the acquaintance of a truly amiable and sensible man.

Haliday's reply was direct and unequivocal: he was not interested in Crosbie's proposal. He cited all the pressing demands on the city's financial resources – establishing a linen industry, dealing with textile competition from Manchester, setting up an educational academy, improving the harbour, maintaining the poorhouse and supporting the Volunteer force. Moreover, Haliday saw no possible benefits of ballooning:

> The mere waste of useful materials which goes into inflating these useless balloons would be a sufficient objection were there none other; for the *cui bono* has never yet, I think, been satisfactorily answered. Let then these light gaudy machines, with superb empty custom-houses and hollow police bills, remain with other vain and costly luxuries in the metropolis, and let poor people be frugal and mind their business … It is high time to desist from these aerial excursions, which only serve to set people a-gazing, when they should be looking attentively on things within, or contiguous to themselves.

In Charlemont's next letter, he was equally direct in expressing his own views on ballooning and yet retained a great admiration and affection for Crosbie the man:

> Perfectly of your mind in all you have said respecting balloons. You have precisely stated my own ideas, though far better expressed than they could have been by me; you have sent me my own thoughts in a Haliday dress. I detest balloons, which I look upon as the silly invention of a trifling age, and, indeed, an excellent sample of those manners which prefer curiosity to use and bubbles to solidity. A boy's kite appears to me as amusing and to the full as useful; but even allowing them all the merit which their greatest favourers would wish to bestow on them, a slight perusal of your Belfast expenses would make any man in his senses devoutly deprecate the diverting of a single shilling to an object so puerile. Go on and prosper, strengthen, enrich and adorn your country by your plans of education and manufactures. Cultivate the elements of earth, fire and water, and leave the air to metropolitan visionaries and idlers. My friendship for Crosbie alone induced me to write to you at his earnest request. He is really an excellent man, and bating his 'balloon-manie,' which he will never get rid of till he

has crossed the channel or drowned himself, is calculated to be a most useful member of society. Upon the receipt of your letter, I sent for him, told him your sentiments and detailed your arguments. He did not – because he could not – make battle; but assured me that many of your citizens had wished for his coming, and had even offered to subscribe largely. How he will determine I know not, but believe that if he should meet with encouragement here he will drop his Belfast scheme. Should he go, I only beg that you would distinguish between him and his balloon; be civil to the one, and as rude as you please to the other. My affection for him, which is really great, has alone induced me to patronise his plans, and every balloon but Crosbie's is odious to me.

This frank exchange of letters is very revealing about Charlemont's general attitude to the balloon craze, and clearly confirms his genuinely warm affection for Crosbie. Coming from a man of Charlemont's standing this was a fine testimonial, and his continuing support for Crosbie in spite of his own instincts, is a clear indication of his high regard for him. Charlemont's lack of enthusiasm for ballooning probably reflected the attitude of many influential figures by this stage. Crosbie was clearly obsessed with the idea of making the balloon crossing to England, and it seems likely that he did not abandon his dream after this setback, but I have not found references to any further efforts by him.

After 1786, Crosbie seems to have disappeared from the pages of Irish history. This is the conclusion of almost all previous accounts of his life, which suggest that his death took place in 1800. However, I have recently established that Richard Crosbie was in New York in 1800, where, *mirabile dictu*, he was once again entertaining the public with a balloon experiment.

9

THE RIVALS

She's as headstrong as an allegory on the banks of the Nile.

Mrs Malaprop, in R.B. Sheridan's *The Rivals*.

Crosbie had three challengers in the period of his balloon experiments in Ireland, beginning with a Scotsman named James Dinwiddie in 1784. The public confrontations between Crosbie and Dinwiddie must have added spice to the race to be the first man to explore the Irish sky. Dinwiddie was the uncle of Riddick, who had sent up a balloon in Dublin in early 1784, and he was an itinerant scientist and philosopher who lectured on a wide range of subjects. He first arrived in Belfast in 1779, and travelled around Ireland for most of the next six years. In Waterford and in Kilkenny in 1784, he successfully demonstrated a small-scale balloon flight during his lectures, and when he arrived in Dublin he advertised his lecture in the Opera House in Capel Street.

Dinwiddie's interests covered diving bells, military and naval battles, transport and engineering, and he always displayed models at his lectures.

During one real experiment with a diving bell, two companions of his died of asphyxiation, while Dinwiddie was waiting in a boat to make his descent after them. In Dublin in 1784, he gave a lecture on electrical experiments, and admission prices ranged from 3s 3d for boxes to 1s 1d for the upper gallery. This lecture was hailed for its 'variety of beautiful electrical experiments, particularly those of a more luminous and transparent nature, which were pleasing beyond description'. Dinwiddies's next lecture was on the diving bell and the air balloon, 'in the first of which, in a real and capacious bell, A BOY will be sent down, and in respect of the latter several balloons will be floated during the lecture'. He also demonstrated an invention called 'a flying chariot' which had nothing to do with balloons. He may have been using the current terminology as a marketing ploy. The invention was in fact a type of 'hobby-horse' or precursor of the bicycle, and Dinwiddie claimed that it would carry two persons at six miles per hour 'without horse or any other power applied, except the feet of one of the travelers'. In May 1785, it travelled around St Stephen's Green with two people on board in under seven minutes. The vehicle was on display in Stokes' Great-Room in Capel Street.

The success of lectures such as Dinwiddie's around the country is an indication of the huge interest in scientific developments of all kinds, supported by advertisements and reports in the press. Dr Linde Lunney's study of Dinwiddie's career tells of his time spent in Ireland, and his conflict with Crosbie.

At one lecture in Dublin, Dinwiddie displayed a model of Crosbie's design, and made disparaging comments on his balloon experiments, without realising that Crosbie was in the audience. Crosbie responded in white heat at the way Dinwiddie had presented his work. He began by saying that he had hurried back from an agreeable party in the country (supporting an impression of him as a *bon vivant*) in order to hear Dinwiddie's lecture:

His purpose, to the disgrace of philosophy, was no other than to depreciate and vilify the endeavours of one who did not stand forward as a professional rival to the lecturer but only wished to make such a use of the little knowledge some experience and observation had given him, in the advancement of a pleasing and scientific pursuit, and who lamented that his private finances were insufficient to enable him to offer his expensive labours to the curious without any other recompense than that most pleasing to the ingenious mind, the applause of a discerning public. My astonishment however did not end here; it increased in no small degree at finding this Professor's scientific principles as erroneous as his private ones are illiberal.

Dinwiddie's 'Flying Chariot'. *Volunteer Journal*, May 1785. (Courtesy of National Library of Ireland.)

It is not my intention to enter into a paper or any other war with this philosophical orator as I flatter myself that my family, my situation and my connections in this my native country place me as far above a thought of this kind, as I trust, the candour and judgement of the public will place my attempts in this branch of speculative and practical science above the reach of disappointed malignity.

Crosbie went on to specify a number of errors of fact made by Dinwiddie in his lecture and tackled each of them. The *Freeman's Journal* at this stage was pro-Crosbie and rallied round 'a native', with high praise for his 'modest, ingenious and well-written letter on the illiberal conduct and erroneous descriptions of Mr. Dinwiddie':

Mr. Crosbie has hitherto amply gratified a discerning public and none of his country men entertains a doubt but he will fully execute what he has pledged to perform. Mr. Dinwiddie was better revise his false philosophy and not attempt under the guise of science to impose on a too generous audience. Let him also learn a little candour and modesty and not use a mean and illiberal effort to lessen the estimation of a respectable gentleman, a native of that kingdom where Mr. Dinwiddie has been suffered to intrude himself and to read lectures which if criticized on by a Crosbie might soon leave him perhaps without character and without bread.

Dinwiddie was also described in the press as 'the hungry Caledonian emigrant'. He replied, denying any intention of vilifying Crosbie, 'I had objects of greater consequence in view, the instruction and entertainment of the public and my own private emolument.' He said that he had devoted only about three minutes of the lecture to Crosbie's ingenious experiments, accusing Crosbie of misquoting what he had said by omitting the crucial word 'not'. 'However trifling a monosyllable it may appear to Mr. Crosbie, I do assure him it is sometimes of great consequence to me, and I now declare that if Mr. Crosbie does *not* quote me more fairly in future, I shall *not* give myself the trouble of replying to him.'

Dinwiddie went on to dismiss other accusations by Crosbie as, 'mere puffs of inflammable air [*which*] prove that Mr. Crosbie's varnish is not so good as he would have us believe'. Referring to Crosbie's assertion of his social status, Dinwiddie wrote, 'He commences an attack on me and then, unsoldierlike, retreats behind the bulwark of his own importance, derived from his family situation and connection.' (This may have been a cutting reference to Crosbie's brief and unsuccessful military career.) Dinwiddie's letter ended with a recommendation to Crosbie to use the shorter Irish Sea crossing from Donaghadee, rather than Dublin. In one respect Dinwiddie was obliged to accept that he had erred in presenting to the audience an incomplete model of Crosbie's aeronautical chariot: he had omitted the masts and sails.

Although Dinwiddie was primarily a lecturer, he moved from theory to practice and constructed a balloon in which he intended to make a flight from Belfast, where he was always very popular. This was planned for July 1785, but in fact it never took place. Dinwiddie left Ireland in late 1785 and later had a very successful career as a scientist in India and China.

DR POTAIN

In early May 1785, on one page of the *Volunteer Journal*, there were advertisements for Dinwiddie's 'flying chariot', Crosbie's flight from Royal Barracks, and a short announcement headed 'Aerial Voyage':

> Doctor Potain most respectfully begs leave to inform the public that on Monday next, he will begin to inflate his BALLOON in Marlborough Green, in which, when finished, he intends CROSSING THE CHANNEL.

Crosbie and Potain, a Frenchman, were working simultaneously towards the same aim, and for a time in the summer of 1785 there was a possibility of a balloon race between the two men. They both used

Ticket of admission to Potain's launch in Dublin. (Courtesy of the Board of Trinity College Dublin.)

the medium of the press to score points: for example when the *Dublin Journal* was reporting on the Royal Barracks debacle, Potain placed a notice in the same paper stating that he had a proper covering on Marlborough Green to display his inflated balloon, and affirming that it was the largest ever seen in Ireland.

There is no specific information on how Potain came to be in Ireland, or if he had previous ballooning experience. He may have wished to surpass the achievement of his fellow-countryman Blanchard by crossing an even wider sea than the English Channel. He arrived in Dublin with letters of recommendation from Benjamin Franklin and the Marquis de Lafayette. These impressed Sir Edward Newenham of Belcamp House, Dublin, who promoted Potain's cause. Newenham was a radical politician in the 1780s, and he was a friend and correspondent of Benjamin

Franklin and George Washington. Potain's publicity involved recording the names of subscribers in books which were located in popular haunts such as the coffee rooms of both Houses of Parliament and The Royal Exchange. He also gave balloon displays in Crow Street Theatre. The coffee houses of Dublin in the eighteenth century were important social centres, mainly for men, and this was Potain's chosen method of gaining publicity and support. Daly's of College Green was one of the best known. Here the young and old could prance and preen, and they were places of bravado and braggadocio. Printers and publishers could rub shoulders with politicians, lawyers, actors and academics, and topical issues were discussed with passion.

No doubt the rivalry between Crosbie and Potain was a source of much debate. Potain's strategy differed from Crosbie's, in that he did not expect to receive any money from subscribers until after the flight had taken place. He actually asked tradesmen to deliver their bills to him in advance as he wished, 'to leave Ireland with that reputation which has hitherto marked his character through life'. After the failure on 10 May at Royal Barracks, Crosbie was encouraged by the *Freeman's Journal* to follow Potain's example, and to make less grandiose claims. It commended Potain's approach as modest and efficient, with no vain boasts or over-confidence. However, the *Dublin Journal* sided with the Irishman, castigating 'the mistaken policy of encouraging every itinerant, to the prejudice of our own natives'. It pointed out that, contrary to his claims, Potain had done nothing to help the Irish economy, since his balloon and all his materials had been imported. The 17 June 1785 was dubbed 'Potain's Day' and he advised shipping vessels about his plan, which suggests that he lacked confidence in his equipment. His balloon had a rudder and a propeller or fly, just like Crosbie's original design and like the one Blanchard used in crossing the English Channel. Potain's wickerwork car weighed 160lbs and was made waterproof by a covering of oil-cloth, by which it might also stay afloat if it finished in the sea. There was also a net inside the car so that it could be cut away from the balloon if required.

Potain secured the support of many formidable figures, among whom were Lord Moira, Lord Edward Fitzgerald, Lord Farnham, Lord Trimbleston, Lord Delvin, Lord Muskerry, Lord Jocelyn, Lord Landaff, Lord Killeen, and the Duke of Leinster. Also on his committee were these prominent men: Sir Richard McGwire, Sir Edward Newenham, Sir James Stratford Tynte, Sir Richard Johnston, Dr Ussher, Hon. John Rawdon, Hon. George Jocelyn, Rt Hon. Thomas Connolly, Mr Whaley, Mr Whaley Jnr, Mr Bell, Mr Baker, Mr Molyneux, Mr Preston, Mr Coddington, Doctor Lynch, Mr Hayes, Mr Ayres, Mr Archibald Hamilton Rowan and Mr Godfrey. These names are recorded as being on the committee on 1 June 1785, when Crosbie's star was at its lowest. Potain must have worked assiduously in winning such widespread support. Two men on his committee were also on Crosbie's at this time: the Duke of Leinster and Sir Richard McGwire. By contrast with Potain, Crosbie had the support of only two peers: Lord Charlemont and Lord Roden. Nevertheless, retaining the support of Charlemont, who is conspicuously absent from Potain's list, was a considerable asset to Crosbie, and further validation of their friendship.

Newspaper reports stated that Potain had initially planned to bring two others with him, two noblemen who wished to keep their names secret until the day. Their names are revealed in Potain's account of his flight: Sir Edward Newenham and his son. They were prevailed upon to abandon their plan by Lady Newenham. She was pregnant with her eleventh child and her distress on hearing of their plans convinced them to change their minds. Benjamin Franklin also wrote to Newenham 'with the anxious freedom of a friend' to dissuade him from attempting the balloon flight. An intrepid young woman was determined to take part and become the first woman in Ireland to fly in a balloon, but Potain declined her request. The woman's name was M.L. O'Reilly, and this letter from her was included in Potain's published account of his time in Ireland:

Sir, If your balloon will take up two I will be happy to accompany you in your aerial excursion as no woman in this Kingdom has hitherto attempted it. The novelty of it may please the Public, be of service to you and give infinite satisfaction to you.

However, Potain ultimately went aloft on his own. From the illustration on the admission ticket, his balloon did have some of the devices which Crosbie had abandoned, such as wings and a type of rudder. The *Freeman's Journal* expressed its satisfaction that he knew exactly when his balloon was sufficiently inflated and so ascended punctually and with no inconvenience or waste of the public's time. He ascended in very high spirits, but was then seen to drift towards the Wicklow Mountains rather than out to sea.

Potain seemed determined not to give any offence or cause for complaint, and reports of him dropping some bizarre pamphlets from his balloon must therefore be regarded as a hoax. In Dixon's article of 1955, these were said to be headed 'CARD to the IRISH NATION' and the text read:

> FINDING your country so corrupted, we wish to visit the Regions of VIRTUE in order to complain to the GODS of your great and increasing degeneracy and to implore their Assistance towards saving a SINKING STATE. ADVERTISEMENT! ADVERTISEMENT! NEWS! NEWS! FROM ABOVE.
> We met the GODS, convened in COUNCIL!
> They resolved THAT prostituted Courtiers, Pseudo Patriots, Calumniators of Irish VOLUNTEERS and the Enemies of the FREEDOM of the PRESS, should never enter the Regions of Eternal Bliss.

Ultimately, Potain's attempt to cross the sea came to an end in the hills above Powerscourt waterfall, in a place called Mullinaveague, near the house of Mrs Price, daughter of Mr Rathborne, a Dublin merchant. What happened was that the hoop around the centre of the balloon damaged the fabric, causing the balloon to descend. Potain was dragged along within feet of the ground for about two miles, but managed to free himself, and the balloon was swept off to Co. Wexford, fifty miles away. He went to a nearby house, but as he could speak no English, he had great difficulty in communicating his predicament until some gentlemen who had been following on horseback from Dublin came along.

Throughout July, notices appeared in the press from Dr Potain, and two supporters named Durry and Osmont about a subsequent launch from Ranelagh Gardens, but the event kept being deferred. Crosbie was then planning his next launch, and the *Freeman's Journal* relished the prospect of a balloon race between the two. The Duchess of Rutland was to launch Potain's balloon on 27 July. However, the event was under-subscribed, and never took place. Potain faced financial ruin, so much so that he was described as starving, and his balloon became a stake for the rent he owed at Ranelagh. He was eventually rescued by one of his compatriots in Dublin, M. Fontaine, a dancing master, who enabled him to return to France. Despite his unfortunate experiences in Ireland, Potain did not hold any grudge, and he published a book in 1824 with the title *Relation Aérostatique, dédiée a la nation Irlandaise*. He was described as '*Ancien Chirugien-Major a la Marine Royale*' and '*Ex-Chirugien Principal d'Armée*'. Perhaps it was his status as Surgeon-General to the French navy and army which ensured that he was well received by the aristocracy of Dublin. His adventure might have been forgotten, were it not for the fact that F.E. Dixon recorded it in his article in *Dublin Historical Record* of 1955. For Potain, it was clearly the outstanding event of his life, as the dedication of his book reveals:

> *A une des plus hospitalièrs Nations de l'Europe.*
> *C'est a vous, Irlandais, que je dois le plus beau moment de ma vie! L'acceuil que vous daignâtes me faire, le généreux empressement que vous mîtes à seconder mon enterprise périlleuse sont pour moi de précieux souvenirs, qui m'encouragent à vous soumettre la Relation de mon voyage aérostatique qui eut lieu à Dublin: puissant mon zèle et ma reconnaissance mériter votre suffrage! C'est le voeu le plus sincère de votre dévoué et très-respectueux serviteur, Dr. Potain.*

(To one of the most hospitable nations of Europe. It is to you Ireland that I owe the most wonderful moment of my life! The welcome which you deigned to offer me, the generous eagerness with which you supported my dangerous enterprise, are for me a precious memory, which encourage me to submit to you the Account of my balloon voyage which began in Dublin; may my zeal and my gratitude merit your approval! This is the very sincere wish of your devoted and very respectful servant, Dr Potain.)

Advertisement for Durry flight. *Volunteer Journal*, April 1786. (© Dublin City Library and Archive.)

MR AND MISS DURRY

An interesting balloon flight was planned from Ranelagh Gardens in April 1786, the same month as Crosbie's Limerick flight, by a brother and sister named Durry. They were English, and Mr Durry had featured in reports in 1785 as a supporter of Potain's ill-fated attempt at a second flight. Miss Durry was no doubt aware that she would be the first woman to fly in Ireland, and she showed a great determination to join those magnificent men in their flying machines. The *Dublin Journal* was supportive, 'When a lady with a spirit superior to that timidity of her sex undauntedly ventures to explore the pathless regions of the air, the lovely aeronaut cannot fail of receiving the warmest encouragement from the sons of Ierne.'

Once again, the roads were thronged with carriages, and by 10a.m. all the fields around Ranelagh were reported to be filled with people. The *Volunteer Journal* said that 'they flocked to the heights like ants to molehills, to every contiguous tree like rooks'. However, there were few people in the garden itself, too few to ensure that the event would cover its costs. The *Freeman's Journal* lamented the fact that so many people stayed in their carriages outside the garden in order to save money – 'a sight very unworthy and an ill-timed piece of economy'. The crowd waited patiently until 4p.m. when the pair finally entered the basket. However, the balloon would not rise, even when all the ballast was thrown out:

> Miss Durry then, with evident reluctance, and with tears in her eyes, was prevailed on to quit the car, to let her brother have the whole honour of the aerial flight – but to his inexpressible mortification, he was still too heavy to be taken up. Impatience now flashed in Miss Durry's countenance, and being considerably lighter than her brother, she prevailed upon him, in turn, to quit the car, with joy and agility leapt into it, and with the utmost intrepidity, and amidst an universal shout of applause, desired the balloon to be liberated. Not a person present but gazed on the little heroine with admiration and astonishment.

In Miss Durry's first attempt, she was almost dashed against a temporary orchestra stand in the garden, and the net of the balloon became entangled. The next time, the balloon bounced along the ground and she was nearly thrown out. After her fourth attempt, she was 'at length compelled with inexpressible regret to quit the phaetonic carriage'. Then a young man from the crowd came forward, stripped to the waist and made one last attempt. He fared worse, becoming entangled in the trees and damaging the balloon fabric. As a consolation to the public, it was then decided to release the unmanned balloon, which eventually came down fifteen miles away in a park owned by Lord Arran. The *Freeman's* account was sympathetic to the pair, but the *Hibernian Magazine* was much less gracious, condemning the whole affair as a fraud, 'So compleat a humbug has not been played off in this or any other kingdom since the days of the never to be forgotten quart-bottle conjuror.' It complimented the patience of the crowd, and the fact that there was no outrage at the scene, although some people had been tempted to attack young Mr Durry.

The event was well attended, but the *Volunteer Journal* reported that, 'the multitude chiefly consisted of persons who had clandestinely got in', and the takings amounted to only £18. It is not surprising perhaps that the Durrys do not feature in any other reports, and it seems that they did not make any more flights. The honour of being the first woman to fly in Ireland was not won until the early years of the nineteenth century.

VINCENT LUNARDI

In England in April 1786, the great Vincent Lunardi was reported as having an interest in crossing the Irish Sea, or St George's Channel, as it was again referred to. He had constructed a new balloon and had experimented on the Thames with it. It had an unusual design:

The shape and neck of this machine are formed on true geometric principles and though its rising power is very great, it can never burst, nor the
small canoe appended to it possibly overset when on the water even were it
ever so much agitated. The canoe is only 18 inches wide and 4 feet long and
made of white iron.

Lunardi came to Dublin in May, and the *Freeman's Journal* welcomed
the prospect of a race between him and Crosbie as 'a *nouvelle spectacle*
in the history of ballooning'. Lunardi's plan was to have a trial inland
flight first, and he proposed to ascend from Rotunda Gardens, prom-
ising to donate his profits to the Lying-in Hospital. This was indeed
a generous gesture towards the struggling institution. However, there
is no evidence that either of his proposed flights took place. It seems
that his reception in Dublin was not as warm as he had expected.
Comparisons were made between him and Crosbie, and one paper
had apparently been critical of Lunardi as a foreigner. The *Freeman's*
response was unequivocal:

As Mr. Lunardi's amazing abilities in every part of the science of aerostation
are so clearly conspicuous, nothing but the most gross and ignorant prejudice will pretend to deny his distinguished superiority.

Lunardi's whole plan seems to have a strong gambling dimension, with
an announcement in London's *Morning Post* that an unidentified man
had wagered £400 that if Lunardi attempted a channel flight, he would
do likewise. In London, wagers amounting to £2,000 were believed to
have rested on the outcome of the flight. There were reports that, after
Dublin, Lunardi had plans to explore tropical regions to seek out the
causes of monsoons and trade winds, and that he would go to northern
Europe and Asia 'to ascertain whether the continents of the old and
new world are divided by water or not'. These stories may have been
no more than attempts to whip up public interest, a ploy not unknown
in modern times. There seems to have been a broad welcome for

Lunardi in the main newspapers, but for whatever reason, he made no flight from Dublin. He tried to organise ascents from Cork and from Belfast, but nothing appears to have come of these either. Lunardi's Irish experience was confirmation that balloon fatigue had taken hold in Dublin, and even further afield perhaps. We can only speculate about whether Crosbie and Lunardi ever met in Dublin or what attitude they adopted towards each other.

10

RICHARD CROSBIE IN AMERICA

He bore the countenance of old Belisarius in all its calm majesty,
but the practiced eye soon found a mind falling into ruin.

A description of Richard Crosbie in 1819.

Very little, if anything, seems to have been published in Ireland about Crosbie's life after his ballooning exploits of 1784-1786. Most sources suggest that he died in 1800, and this was given some credence by the comment of his friend Jonah Barrington that 'he died too early for science and for friendship'. However, Tom Cranitch has added some further fascinating information from Barrington showing that he later revised this view:

It has since been discovered that death did not master him for many years. His history is not a common one. I have lately received a considerable quantity of documents and manuscripts collected or written during the period he was supposed to be dead and at many different places till a late day. Most of them are to me utterly unintelligible; but there is sufficient to furnish matter for one of the most curious memoirs that can be conceived and altogether novel. So multifarious, however, are the materials that I fear their due arrangement would be quite beyond my powers.

It would be very useful to find out whether these documents given to Barrington are still extant, but I have found no further clues. There has been great mystery about the last years of Crosbie's life and about his death. At an early stage in this research, I came across two specific references to a precise date for his death in Dublin. The first was in an on-line source, a list of deaths in *The Asiatic Journal and Monthly Miscellany,* Vol. 18, 1824, 'In Nth. Cumberland St., Dublin in his 68th year, Richard Crosbie Esq., youngest son of the late Sir Paul Crosbie, Bart., of the County of Wicklow.' Then I found confirmation of this intriguing information in an article by Larry Walsh in *The Old Limerick Journal*, quoting Maurice Lenihan's *History of Limerick* (1866):

> May 30th 1824: Died in Dublin, Richard E. Crosbie, Esq., aged 68 years; the first who ascended in a balloon in Dublin or anywhere else. He ascended from the rere of the House of Industry, on the North Strand, on the 27th of April, 1786.

I have not, however, succeeded in finding other death notices or obituaries in newspapers of the day. This is ironic, since newspapers of the 1780s found so much that was newsworthy in Crosbie's exploits. Fascinated by these brief references, I became convinced that there was more material to be uncovered about Crosbie's later career. By virtue of the treasure trove of information provided by on-line sources, I have found confirmation of this. The first success came in a search of the digital archive of *The Irish Times,* in a news item of 17 September 1910, headed 'First Flight over the Irish Channel: History repeats itself'. The following is the first paragraph:

FIRST FLIGHT OVER THE IRISH CHANNEL.

HISTORY REPEATS ITSELF.

History has once more repeated itself, but with a curious reversal of the order of things. Ireland's first aeronaut, Richard Crosbie, of Crosbie Park, County Wicklow, the first to make the attempt to cross the Channel in a balloon, ended his days as an actor on the American stage. And now Mr. Robert

From *The Irish Times* Digital Archive, 17 September 1910.

History has once more repeated itself, but this time with a curious reversal of the order of things. Ireland's first aeronaut, Richard Crosbie, of Crosbie Park, Co. Wicklow, the first to make the attempt to cross the channel in a balloon, ended his days as an actor on the American stage. And now, Mr. Robert Loraine, after a distinguished career on the boards, both at home and abroad, has established a record by flying on his bi-plane from Holyhead to the coast of Howth.

This little nugget of information was the first reference I had ever come across to an acting career for Crosbie, or to America. It was a stimulus to further exploration. The result was confirmation in several other sources that Crosbie did indeed tread the boards in America. One of these is the *Freeman's Journal* of 30 May 1924, which also confirmed the date of his death:

In 1792, he turned actor and went to New York, where he appeared in a number of characters, but returned to Ireland in the early nineteenth century and died in Dublin on May 30th, 1824.

The search results were more fruitful when the variant spelling 'Crosby' was used for the surname, and I found that an actor called 'Sir Richard Crosby' appeared in the results. The first Crosby reference dates from New York in December 1793, and mentions that he was also known as

Mr. Richards. The name occurs in the records of John Street Theatre in New York, which closed down in 1797. This unflattering account of Crosbie's first stage appearance and of his acting ability is from *A History of the American Theatre from its Origins to 1832*, written by William Dunlap:

> On the 28th December Sir Richard Crosby made his appearance in the character of Barbarossa. He was announced as Mr. Richards but after some time resumed his name of Crosby, dropping the distinguishing mark of his nobility. He was by birth and education a gentleman and spoke his parts with propriety but his face was that of a species called pudding and his person literally gigantic without any of those swelling contours which render the Hercules Farnese so admirable. The contours of Crosby were all misplaced and might remind a spectator of Foote's description of a nobleman of his day – 'he looks like a greyhound that has the dropsy.' Crosby was some inches in height over 6 foot and like many men who are conscious of being tall he sunk instead of elevating his head and 'the stride of the tyrant' was reduced to a gait and a trot and a pace. That with all this against him he should remain on the stage and be tolerated is one of the proofs of the triumph of mind over matter. He was not likely to rival either of the managers or the managers' manager and he was supported behind the curtain and in the journals of the day. This gentleman was an Irishman; he dissipated a fortune among the claret drinkers of the land of hospitality, had built a balloon, ascended in it, and like the ambitious high flying Greek had fallen into the sea. Sir Richard Crosby had been picked up by some fishing boats in the Irish channel, and preserved to fall, alien to his caste, a poor actor on the stage of the old American company.

Another book, *Records of the New York Stage*, by Joseph Norton Ireland, gives this account:

> Richards was the assumed designation of Sir Richard Crosby, an Irish baronet, whom reverses of fortune had thrown upon the stage. His height was more than 6 feet but his face was inexpressive, and his bearing the reverse of majestic. His manners however were those of a gentleman, and as he had the

advantage of a good education, his readings were correct if hot-spirited, and in serious old men in his latter days he was always respectable. After the first season or two he resumed his surname of Crosby, without the prefix Sir. He returned to England and died there in 1806.

Yet another reference is even more succinct and conflates the sequence of events in a dramatic fashion. It is from *Chronology of the American Stage* by Francis Courtney Wemyss:

> Sir Richard Crosby: an English baronet who became an actor in a most romantic manner, having made an ascent in a balloon, he descended into the sea, was picked up and carried to New York where, at the John St. Theatre, he made his first appearance on the American stage, 28th December 1793, as Barbarossa.

Notwithstanding some garbling of the facts, these accounts clearly refer to the Irish aeronaut. It seems likely that Crosbie left Ireland because he was obliged to face a mountain of debt and the prospect of a jail term as a debtor. It was a flight of a different kind for him. He must have decided that a prison term was to be avoided at all costs and that his much-vaunted family credentials were not enough to save him. He began by making an effort to conceal his identity as 'Mr Richards' but in time must have become more secure and reverted to his own name, with a variation on the spelling. Assuming the title 'Sir' undoubtedly gave him a special status among the thespians of the new world, and perhaps it was his way of redressing the wrong done in not being honoured after his exploits in 1785. He could also say that it was only an accident of birth that prevented him from acquiring the title held by his older brother.

Crosbie's financial troubles are explicitly alluded to in an account in French of 1834. The source is *Revue Brittanique*:

> *On vit meme sur la planche de New York un rejeton d'une des plus nobles familles irlandaises, Sir Richard Crosby, autrefois propriétaire d'un beau chateau dans l'ile de Erin, et qui après avoir sacrificié a son penchant gastronomique les domains légués*

*par ses aieux, s'avisa de fabriquer un ballon, voulut passer la Manche et tomba dans
la mer avec son aérostat. Recueilli par quelques pecheurs de la cote, mais pour-suivi
presque aussitot par ses créanciers, il se hata de passer en Amérique, ou sa taille
cotrefaite, son ventre tuméfié et ses longues jambes d'araignée ne l'empechèrent pas de
jouer les heros et d'avoir du succès.*

(One also saw on the New York stage a descendant of one of the most
noble Irish families, Sir Richard Crosby, former owner of a beautiful
castle in the island of Erin, and who, having lost the estates bequeathed
to him by his forefathers due to his fondness for good food and wine,
decided to construct a balloon in which he wished to cross the Channel
and fell into the sea with his flying-machine. Rescued by some fisher-
men on the coast, but immediately pursued by his creditors, he quickly
made his way to America, where his ill-formed figure, his swollen
stomach and his long spidery legs did not prevent him from playing
heroic roles and achieving success.)

John Hodgkinson was the manager of John Street Theatre, and
there are several on-line references to plays in which Crosbie played
various parts. In 1793, he played in *The Carmelite* and in 1796, he
played 'Walter' in a musical based on *The Vicar of Wakefield* by Oliver
Goldsmith. He had small parts in *As You like It, Much Ado about Nothing*
and numerous other plays in 1797, before the theatre closed its doors.
Many of the parts he played were in plays by Irish authors, such as
Love a la Mode by Charles Macklin, in which he played Sir Callaghan
O'Brallaghan. A play called *The Poor Soldier* was staged in September
1797 for the benefit of Crosbie. There is a supreme irony in finding
Crosbie playing a role in this very popular comic opera by Irish author
John O'Keeffe, who wrote in his *Recollections* that he had set the play
around Carton, the seat of the Duke of Leinster - the man who had
been one of Crosbie's staunch supporters and whose two sons, Henry
and Edward, had chased the balloon from Royal Barracks. By coincidence, Lord Henry Fitzgerald became a successful actor in Dublin
for a period in the 1790s. Crosbie must surely have been aware of the

irony, and the references to Leixlip and Carton must have brought back poignant memories of his old life, as would these lines, sung by the poor soldier:

> Be gentlemen fine with their spears and nice boots on
> Their horses to start on the Curragh of Kildare
> Or dance at the ball with their Sunday new suits on
> Lac'd waistcoats, white gloves and their nice powdered hair.

Crosbie had been a member of the Benevolent Theatre Society in Dublin, and he may have been an actor before leaving for America, probably around 1792. He must have found that acting was the best way of making a living in the United States. During his time as a jobbing actor, Crosbie found himself in a prison cell for one night in Boston. There were no charges against him, but his night in the cells must have been the nadir of his career.

The on-line diary of William Dunlap for 1797-98, refers to Crosbie's financial troubles. This is the first reference, 'Endeavouring to settle Crosbie's business. I have offered to pay 50 *d*s more for him rather than surrender the wretch to a jail.' Dunlap then gives an account of the circumstances in which Crosbie and a fellow actor named Collins came to spend a night in the cells, as reported to him in a letter from Hodgkinson:

> Collins having ill-treated his wife and seduced or attempted to seduce Mrs King discharged the Company, and finding that [Richard] Crosbie had mentioned some part of his conduct, he challenged him; the duel was prevented by [Joseph] Tyler's informing the magistrates and the heroes, after lieing in jail from Sunday evening to Monday were examined, Crosbie dismissed and Collins re-committed for trial, but afterwards liberated on condition of quitting the state.

This diary entry was written in New York in 1797:

Running about to see and borrow money and settle the unfortunate debt
contracted for Crosbie. Settle Crosbie's affair.

In 1798, Dunlap made this entry:

As to Crosby's affair, it is very probable I could not substantiate any debt
against Mr. H. for money paid to relieve him (Crosby). I relied on a sense of
justice in Mr. H. Don't you who know him, laugh at me?

There was apparently a dispute between Dunlap and Hodgkinson over
money advanced to Crosbie. Hodgkinson wrote as follows to a third
party, and the letter is quoted by Dunlap:

Mr. Dunlap cannot charge me with anything respecting Crosby, because
since the transaction he has signed him a general release, and at the time,
took the affair on himself.

As an untalented actor playing minor roles with a struggling theatre
company, Richard Crosbie, the cynosure of Dublin in 1785, the man
who had been hailed in ballads as 'the true Columbus of the trackless
air' and 'Hibernia's favoured son,' had truly suffered the fate of Icarus.
His on-going financial difficulties are not explained but they may have
been caused by an enterprise of his which came to fruition in 1800,
and which had a direct link with his glory years in Ireland.

A brief on-line reference led me to explore reports of a balloon
experiment in New York, and what I found, with the generous assistance of New York Public Library, is quite amazing. A Frenchman
called Joseph Corré set up a pleasure park and a theatre called Mount
Vernon Garden in New York, 'in Leonard Street, two streets above the
hospital'. In addition to the natural attractions, there were fountains,
flying horses and swings. In order to outdo a rival named Delacroix
who was in the same business, Corré devised a plan for a balloon
launch from his garden in the autumn of 1800. There is no trace of

Mount Vernon Garden today but it was located in lower Manhattan, at the north-west corner of Leonard Street and Broadway. Today there is a nightclub near the location.

Ballooning was a relative novelty in America. A thirteen-year-old boy named Edward Warren had ascended in a tethered balloon in Baltimore in 1784, but the first manned flight in America was achieved by Jean Pierre Blanchard on 9 January 1793. It took place from the then capital, Philadelphia, watched by President George Washington and the French ambassador. It was Blanchard's forty-fifth flight, and he covered a distance of fifteen miles, landing in Gloucester County, New Jersey. In an effort to ensure that the public paid to see the launch, it was held inside the walls of a former prison. Despite his best efforts to muster up support, Blanchard's takings fell far short of his expenses. It was reported that 40,000 people witnessed the launch, but most of them were outside. Blanchard was determined to organise another flight, and stayed on in America for the next four years. He went to Charleston, Boston and finally New York in 1796. He had great difficulty in rais-ing funds to clear his debt and this stalled his plans for a second flight. One of his schemes was to fly small tethered balloons with animal pas-sengers. These had parachutes attached and a fuse would release the parachutes automatically; the animals would then drop safely back to earth. Blanchard's time in America brought tragedy: his sixteen-year-old son was killed in a fall from a roof during a storm in New York. To add to his woes, his former partner in crossing the English Channel, Dr John Jeffries, sued him for $370 and won. It is not clear what this case was about. Blanchard returned to France in 1797, and continued to make balloon flights until his death in 1809.

Since Blanchard and Crosbie were in New York at the same time in 1796-97, it is possible that their paths crossed. At the very least, Crosbie must have been aware of the arrival in the town of his former rival. Blanchard's experiments may have rekindled his interest in ballooning and opened up possibilities for him again. In any case, Joseph Corré and Richard Crosbie collaborated in organising balloon events in

Mount Vernon Garden in 1800. At that time New York was considerably smaller than Dublin, with a population of only about 60,500.

The first stage involved lectures and experiments on the science of ballooning presented by Crosbie, in which he demonstrated the process of filling balloons with inflammable air. These lectures took place in Adams Hotel, William Street. Corré's promotional strategy generated a lot of interest among the public and prompted Richard Crosbie to publish this notice in the *Daily Advertiser* of New York on 3 October 1800:

Aerostation.

Mr Crosby.

Encouraged by the favorable manner in which the trifling experiments he made a few nights hence at Mount Vernon Gardens were received by the scientific part of the spectators, and being solicited by many of them to commence a course of experiments in Natural Philosophy, particularly in the science of Aerology & practice of Aerostation: he takes the liberty of informing the public that he is now preparing an Apparatus, and purposes to have the honor of exhibiting some favorite experiments in the course of the next weeks; the time and place will be announced in future advertisements.

His principal view from this undertaking is to accomplish the means of making an Aerial Excursion in this country for philosophical purposes; to obtain which he wishes to lay his plan before the people, and convince them of the delight as well as utility that may be derived from a regular cultivation of this infant science.

Should he be so fortunate as to reap those laurels which he is convinced must one time spring from the important pursuit, he is ambitious of sharing them with the generous and spirited public that may stimulate it, when other parts of the world, satisfied with enjoying it as a wonderful and magnificent spectacle, neglect the applications of it to useful purposes and the improvement of the noblest branch of natural philosophy.

He is aware that the generosity of the public in their liberal efforts to encourage such an exhibition in this city as a curiosity, has been hitherto abused; he will not presume to think such unwarrantable conduct was meditated by those who have been so unfortunate as to disappoint their expectations; but the plan he means to propose must remove from him every shadow of suspicion on that account, which skepticism has a right to cast on other adventurers.

Clearly, Crosbie's ultimate aim was to organise a manned flight from New York. He also continued to believe in the practical scientific benefits to be derived from the science of aerostation, while not under-estimating the sheer pleasure of the magnificent spectacle. Crosbie also refers to some way in which the generosity of the public had been abused, and he wishes to distance himself from 'other adventurers' who seem to have disappointed the public. Could he be referring to Blanchard here? Three years had elapsed since Blanchard had been in New York, but I have not read of any other balloonists in the city during this period. It seems possible, even likely, that he was referring to Blanchard, and that he was determined to succeed where his old rival had failed.

The next newspaper mention of Crosbie was in the *Daily Advertiser* of 27 October 1800, and the announcement has many echoes of those far-off autumn days of his first balloon experiments in Ranelagh Gardens in 1784. Crosbie must have privately reminisced about those heady days, when dukes, lords, ladies and the Dublin public graced his balloon events. Once again, Crosbie was sending small animals aloft, and it is amazing to note that he was allowing only thirty minutes for the inflation process:

Balloon To Be Launched

According to Mr. Crosby's promise to those who attended his lecture and experiments last Tuesday evening, and to convey an idea of the magnificence of an ascent to those who have never seen one, he will liberate his beautiful varnish'd Silk Balloon and Aeronautic carriage, with a living cat or dog, from Mount Vernon Garden THIS DAY the 27th inst. (weather permitting) precisely at half past 3 o'clock.

To remove any apprehensions of disappointment, should the weather prove favorable, further Notice will be given through the city a few hours before the Launching by Proclamation and the sound of a Horn.

N.B. For the satisfaction of those Ladies and Gentlemen who would desire to see the curious Process of filling the balloon with inflammable air, they are respectfully informed the inflation will begin at 3 o'clock.

Admittance to the Promenade above the Boxes, half a Dollar each, to the area below, a quarter of a Dollar.

Tickets or Checks delivered on the night of Lectures will be admitted.

This flight took place only a half hour behind schedule, and a short account of it appeared in the *Daily Advertiser* of 30 October:

Last Monday, about 4 o'clock in the afternoon, a beautiful Balloon, under the direction of Mr. Richard Crosby, was launched from Mount Vernon Gardens, as a specimen of his knowledge of the grand science of Aerology. The wind being light at N. it rose about 400 feet almost perpendicular; then took a southerly course and moved magnificently grand through the atmosphere till it was fairly out of sight. At the bottom of the Balloon was suspended a beautiful Car with a label fastened to it, 'that if any person should pick it up to preserve it for Mr. C. the inventor.'

The ascension was highly satisfactory to the numerous spectators that were present, and did great credit to Mr. Crosby, who we understand proposes to make an aerial voyage in the month of January next, provided the liberality of the public is sufficient to defray the expence.

I have not traced any accounts of further flights organised by Crosbie, and it seems that the liberality of the public did not provide adequate funding for his planned aerial voyage. Nevertheless, it is wonderful to see that he had escaped the tedium and humiliation of minor acting roles and once more, however briefly, had become the leading man of a balloon spectacle. It is remarkable that he had not abandoned his passion, and that he continued to pursue his dream of flight in the belief that ballooning could entertain and bring practical benefits. These short reports suggest that, after his acting career ended, he might have made his living from lecturing on ballooning science and performing practical experiments. There is a possibility that, since his experiments were so well received in New York, he repeated them in other American cities, but I have not come across any further such reports. He was certainly capable of, at least, lecturing on aerostation, even if he did not always have the funds for demonstrations or actual flights.

There are questions about how the unsuccessful and impoverished actor advanced to a position of being able to organise a balloon event for 'numerous spectators' in New York in 1800. He would have had to surmount the same technical and logistical problems as he had in Ireland, and would have needed considerable funds to defray the expense involved. It is tempting to speculate that his debt problems while he was an actor might have arisen out of his dogged determination to organise a balloon flight. If so, then perhaps it was his dream of accomplishing a flight in the new world that sustained him through the humiliating years as an actor. Perhaps future research will help to clarify these issues.

We can only wonder about Crosbie's links with home and family at this time, and how much he might have known of events in Ireland in the 1790s. At that period, many leading figures of the United Irishmen took refuge in America. There was a group of these men in Philadelphia in 1795, and Crosbie would have been familiar with them, possibly even friendly with some of them, in Dublin: Theobald Wolfe Tone, James Napper Tandy, Dr James Reynolds, and Archibald Hamilton Rowan.

The Rising of 1798 had a tragic impact on Richard Crosbie's family, with his brother Edward being executed in June. It is ironic that 1800 is the year suggested in many accounts as the date of Crosbie's death, when, in fact, he was alive and well and repeating his experiments with success and acclaim before an appreciative audience in New York. The story does not end in New York, however, and there is one further dramatic description of an older Richard Crosbie, and an intriguingly brief reference to his adventures in other parts of the world. This comes from a lengthy journal article held in the archives of the University of Michigan and available on the website of Hathi Trust Digital Library.

It provides yet more astonishing details of the declining years of the engineering genius.

The article is entitled 'A Masonic Incident in the Early History of Baltimore' and it relates an experience in the life of General George H. Stuart of Baltimore, Maryland, when he was a young man. In the winter of 1819, he and his brother noticed an old man living in a lean-to or shanty in an alleyway in the east of the city. The man could be seen working with tools and crouching over a small fire, but his shelter was very basic and open to the elements. The brothers were moved to offer

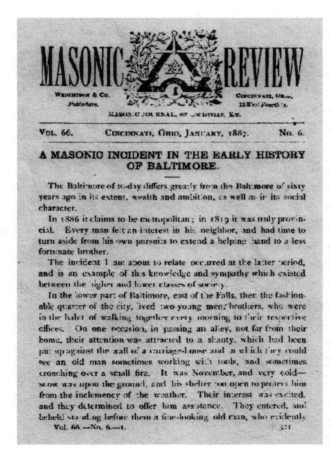

Masonic Review article of 1887.

him some assistance. They approached to find that he was 'a fine looking man, who evidently had seen better days. He was over six feet in height, large in proportion, with a grand head, nearly bald, his snow-white hair falling on his neck.' He was dressed in nankeen trousers and wore slippers, but his un-stockinged feet were swollen with dropsy. He wore an old dress-coat, buttoned to the neck. 'His bearing was that of a dignified gentleman, too proud to tell his needs, and yet gracious in acknowledging kindness. He bore the countenance of old Belisarius in all its calm majesty, but the practiced eye soon found a mind falling into ruin,' wrote the unidentified author of the article. (Belisarius was a Byzantine general under Emperor Justinian.) The brothers initially found that the old man's aloof manner prohibited them from offering him charity.

Observing that the man was visited by a local blacksmith, a Scotsman, Stuart asked him what he knew. The smith told them that he did not know where the old man came from, but that he was the most learned person he had ever met, spoke many languages and was an amateur mechanic and a philosopher. He was working ceaselessly on a model of perpetual motion, and by means of what he termed 'the hydrostatic paradox,' the old man was on the brink of a major discovery, according to the blacksmith. Perpetual motion was a chimera pursued by eccentric scientists of the nineteenth century. It was conceived as a device or system which could constantly generate more energy than it consumed. The principle of conservation of energy, as later expressed in the first law of thermodynamics, implied that such a device was an impossibility, because energy cannot be created or destroyed. This has never been a deterrent to the passionate seekers of a breakthrough. The hydrostatic paradox is defined as the proposition that any quantity of water, however small, may be made to counterbalance any weight, however great, or, alternatively, the law of the equality of pressure of fluids in all directions.

The smith helped to provide the old engineer with brass and iron for his model, by which he was utterly consumed. Sometimes the man would earn a little money by doing small carpentry jobs, but resented any time spent away from his beloved model. The smith feared for the man's life because of his poverty and the extreme cold; at night he lay on his workbench with little covering. The brothers asked to see the model and were impressed by it, saying that it came nearer the achievement of perpetual motion than any other they had seen.

The smith also told the Stuarts that the engineer was a Freemason, as they were, and this gave them the opportunity to offer him the support that was his right according to the fellowship of the Craft. This time he softened, accepted their help, and was provided with clothing and a comfortable room of his own where he could continue to work on 'his darling invention,' which he believed to be near perfection. The account continues:

> After a few days more of intercourse his gratitude expressed itself in tears and he opened his heart to his benefactors, who then heard with astonishment that he was Sir Richard Crosby (or Crosbie), an Irishman, of an old, rich and influential family. He had been educated at the Dublin University, where he had distinguished himself in the study of natural science, making some useful inventions. When twenty years of age he engaged with Montgolfier (the earliest aeronaut in perfecting balloons) and with that distinguished philosopher started from the coast of France on an aerial voyage across the channel, an account of which is given in the Gentlemen's Magazine of the year 1785, where we read that both adventurers were dropped into the sea, and would have drowned but for the exertions of the fishermen who happened to be near the scene.

Although the facts are inaccurate in some respects, there is no doubting that the old man was indeed the Irish airman, whose declining mental faculties, or perhaps the recollections of the Stuarts, or of the author of the article, may have been the cause of the inaccurate details. It was an astonishing discovery for the Stuart brothers, matched by my amazement on reading the account of the last years of Richard Crosbie. Ever the man of surprises, Crosbie's story does not end in 1786 or in 1800, but can now be continued.

There are even more intriguing elements because the article goes on to say that Crosbie had lived an adventurous life in India, South America and in the western wilds of North America, working variously as a teacher, a mechanic, a porter and a boatman on the Mississippi, 'sometimes in good fortune, sometimes in poverty, but always hoping to gain the great prize he had in view'. The 'great prize' is not specified, and one must wonder whether it was to do with perpetual motion or with human flight. The account says that he had married early in life and had one daughter, but there is no mention of his son.

Unfortunately, there are no further details on these picaresque adventures, but this source is confirmation that the papers, recorded by Barrington as being 'most curious memoirs' written in many different places, were indeed genuine. The Stuarts learned that Crosbie had had no contact with his family for thirty years, and had led a dissipated life of gambling and racing. As Crosbie was beginning to open up emotionally among his new friends in Baltimore, some rich Irish merchants there, who were discreetly supporting him, expressed a wish to visit him. Crosbie declined to see them, saying that by his conduct he had cut himself off from his own age and class. 'You young men,' he said to the Stuart brothers, 'are as children to me; toward you I feel differently.' He was a proud man, and perhaps the same 'mortification' which had so often accompanied his enterprises in Ireland was still a powerful emotion for him.

George Stuart then made contact with someone he refers to as 'Lord C.' in Dublin to inform him of the discovery of Richard Crosbie. He does not say why he took this initiative, but it may have been suggested by Crosbie himself. A reply came sixty days later, the length of time it took for two Atlantic crossings. It was an enthusiastic and grateful welcome for the astounding news, a guarantee of financial support and a strong assurance of a warm welcome home for Crosbie in Dublin. Stuart says that Lord C. was a nephew of Crosbie's. My surmise is that Lord C. was Lord Charlemont, the son of Crosbie's patron in 1784, whose residence was in Marino, but there is no evidence that he and Crosbie were related. On the other hand, Stuart may be referring to Richard Crosbie's nephew, Sir

William, 6th Baronet, whose residence was probably in Crosbie Park, Co. Wicklow, but who may have had a town house in Dublin.

Ultimately, Richard Crosbie made the return journey to Dublin in the spring of 1820, sailing via Liverpool. The account says that he received the welcome of the prodigal son in Dublin, and gives his age as eighty. This is not accurate, as Crosbie was only about sixty-four, but he may well have looked eighty. According to the Freemason author, Crosbie was profoundly influenced by what he calls 'the poison derived from the writings of Voltaire, Rousseau and other freethinkers of that day', but that at the end of his life God softened Crosbie's heart, first by gratitude, then by love, and finally by faith and hope. 'He lived two or three years after his return, and then calmly passed away, surrounded by his kindred and friends.' This timescale roughly fits in with the reports of Crosbie's death in 1824.

The article does not end with Crosbie's death. General Stuart and 'Lord C.' remained in correspondence, and in 1850, some thirty years after Crosbie's return to Ireland, Stuart visited Dublin. He asked his unidentified host if he had ever heard of Crosbie, and the man replied that he well remembered Crosbie's triumphal return to Dublin, after he had been presumed dead for many years. The host was only ten at the time, but described it as great day for the Masons, with Crosbie receiving a hero's welcome outside the city, and brought in an open carriage in procession through triumphal arches amid cheering throngs. I have been unsuccessful in finding any references to this event in the newspapers of the time, and a search of the records of the Grand Lodge of Ireland in Dublin has revealed nothing either.

General Stuart was encouraged by his host to visit Lord C., who was described as living only a mile from Dublin. This would correspond with Marino, seat of Lord Charlemont. Stuart walked out there, met a fine-looking old gentleman who embraced him as a brother, saying:

God has been good in letting us meet, for I can never tell you how much we all owe to you and your brother. Our faith in God's promises were almost shaken, as year by year, his old mother waited, believing that her prayers would be answered and he brought back to his home, and at last dying, still trusting. To the younger ones her belief and trust appeared like the imbecility of old age, until the return of her son made her faith a reality.

Francis William Caulfeild, 2nd Lord Charlemont, the son of Crosbie's patron in the 1780s, was born in 1775 and was seventy-five years of age when Stuart visited Dublin. He presumably was the man Stuart visited a mile outside the city. The Masons of Dublin wished to give Stuart a civic reception, but his itinerary did not allow it. The anonymous author of the article adds that Richard Crosbie's daughter, by now an old lady, travelled over a hundred miles to meet him, to thank him for all he had done for her father. She is described as 'a distinguished authoress'. This poses yet another mystery: I have not found any female author of that time named Crosbie. She may have written under a married name or an assumed name.

It would be wonderful to have the details of the above accounts of Crosbie's years in America confirmed, and to find out more about his travels in other locations. Perhaps this will be accomplished by future research. At present, the little that is known about his affairs after he left Ireland confirms Crosbie's determination and dedication to his dream. It is pleasing to learn that his final years were spent in comfort among his own people and in his own home in North Cumberland Street. These anonymous lines, called 'The Balloonist's Prayer', are said to have been adapted from an old Irish sailors' prayer, and are beautifully appropriate to Richard Crosbie's return to Ireland:

The winds have welcomed you with softness.
The sun has greeted you with its warm hands,
You have flown so high and so well
That God has joined you in laughter,
And set you back gently
Into the loving arms of mother Earth.

11

THE CONQUEST
OF THE IRISH SEA

To preserve to the family the honour of terminating
an undertaking … and fixing the undisputed palm of
pre-eminence in the practical application of Aerostation.

Windham Sadler

James Sadler, a chemist, was the son of a confectioner in High Street,
Oxford, and he became the first Englishman to fly in a balloon in
October 1784, just weeks after Lunardi. Like Crosbie, he was an enthusiast and a prodigy, and he designed and constructed his own balloons.
He was architect, engineer, chemist, deviser and pilot in all his flights –
just as Crosbie was. Sadler made seven ascents in total during 1784-85.
He planned to cross the English Channel in late 1784, but his balloon
was destroyed in transit to Dover: the envelope had been folded, and he
found that the varnish had fused the folded sections together. In May
1785, Sadler made a balloon voyage of over fifty miles, from Manchester
to Pontefract, but was badly injured when the car was dragged over two

RURAL SPORTS BALLOON HUNTING.

A cartoonist's view of the impact of balloons. Thomas Rowlandson, 1811.
(Courtesy of the Board of Trinity College Dublin.)

miles along the ground as he tried to land. He had another scare after
a flight from Worcester in the autumn. Attempting to land in a squall
near Lichfield, he was dragged over five miles in the basket. He succeeded in jumping out, but the balloon took off, never to be recovered.
Following these escapes from death, Sadler turned away from ballooning to concentrate on improvements to the steam engine.

At the age of fifty-seven, Sadler returned to ballooning with his two
sons. He attempted a flight from Bristol in 1810, which may have been
an actual attempt to cross the Irish Sea, or a rehearsal for it; either way,
Sadler finished up in the sea and was rescued. In October 1811, he
completed a dramatic flight from Birmingham to Lincolnshire, when
he covered 112 miles in eighty minutes, probably a record speed for

the time. Once again he was feared dead when he was thrown out of the basket at the end. An Irish Sea crossing from Dublin to Liverpool, approximately 100 miles, was his next adventure. Such a journey had not been attempted since Crosbie's flight from Leinster Lawn, twenty-seven years earlier. Sadler was well received in Dublin, and was invited to the homes of many prominent citizens; his plan was described as 'one of the grandest designs ever conceived,' and there was great confidence in his ability to succeed. The following details are from the *Freeman's Journal*.

Sadler's balloon was 55ft in diameter, with a capacity of 87,114 cubic feet, and he carried eleven hundredweight of ballast. He displayed it in the Rotunda Rooms, as Crosbie had done, charging 1s 3d for admission. Newspapers greeted his plan with the same awe as they had greeted Crosbie's in the 1780s, but, inexplicably, without any acknowledgement of Crosbie. The *Journal* commented:

> The amazing project of Mr Sadler to cross the Irish Sea in a balloon will, or we are much mistaken, hand his name down to the latest posterity if he should be able to accomplish his surprising voyage. There is no instance of any attempt that can be paralleled with it.

The only reference to earlier attempts was a rather veiled one: the epilogue marking Crosbie's achievements, which was delivered after the performance of *The Rivals* in 1785, was reprinted.

Sadler's balloon was made of lute-string silk, in strips of crimson and white, and richly decorated. The light car was suspended to a hoop of cane, which was attached by twenty-four ropes to a net made of Italian hemp, covering the whole balloon. Everything was highly ornate, as detailed in the following description:

> The car is also extremely rich, as well in its decoration as in the classical-ity of its design; the shape is oval, and the colour a sea-green; on either side is a representation of the Irish harp, with figures finely modelled; the

upper panels are rendered peculiarly elegant by the insertion of a brass fret-work railing, bordered with crimson; at the head and stem are two Dolphins supporting festoons of oak and ivy; the interior is lined with crimson and cushions to correspond; under the seat are lockers for the purpose of containing ballast &c. This splendid vehicle is attached by six gilt ropes to the base of a dome, on the embellishment of which neither expense nor pains have been spared; it is made of crimson silk intersected with spiral wreaths of oak and laurel; at the top is a rich Ducal coronet; around the base are shamrocks entwined with stars, below which hang a luxuriant drapery of crimson and yellow silk, trimmed with gold fringe formed of acorns and fancifully held with gold crimson tassels by the beaks of eagles, making altogether as elegant an object as imagination can conceive.

A fine colour print confirms the details of the above descriptions, and shows that the barge was named *Erin go Brah*. It has Sadler waving two flags, one of which depicts the Three Castles of Dublin, and the other seems to be the Irish harp. Poolbeg Lighthouse and the South Wall appear in the background, although The print is not accurate, as his course did not in fact take him over those landmarks, but rather over Ireland's Eye. On 1 October 1812, the fifty-nine-year-old James Sadler set off from the grounds of Belvedere House in Drumcondra, Dublin, now St Patrick's College of Education. The house was owned by Mr Beresford, and the ground-floor rooms were reserved for the Duke of Richmond and friends. A military guard was there to keep order, but nothing untoward happened. There were two military bands and several marquees were erected in case of rain. Twenty-seven bottles of oil of vitriol (sulphuric acid) were consumed in the process of filling the balloon, at a cost of £3 10s a bottle. Another detail given was that the weight of the vitriol used was 4,119lbs. The Duchess of Richmond and Lady Sarah Lennox each presented a flag to Sadler before he launched, and one of his sons assisted.

The description of the event suggests that the magic and awe of human flight once again enraptured the public:

James Sadler over Poolbeg Lighthouse, 1812. (Courtesy of the Board of Trinity College Dublin.)

The balloon was released and the undaunted voyager floated from the stage, majestically rising from the Earth on the bosom of the Air, and presenting a spectacle at once awful and sublime, which as it mocks description so was its effect attested by the unbidden tears that stole down many a cheek – for a moment all was silent ecstasy and tremulous fear followed by bursts of applause, not drawn forth by factitious circumstances, but excited by real and undisguised admiration ... If the earnest wishes of above a hundred thousand souls who have been witnesses of his intrepid ascent can have influence over his destiny, his family and friends shall have no occasion to lament his temerity.

Among the spectators were Richard Lovell Edgeworth and his novelist daughter Maria. Edgeworth was a scientist who took a keen interest in the development of the science of aerostation. He is credited by Hodgson with making a significant contribution to the science by proposing that a plane surface, such as might be found by a cloth stretched between rods, would make balloons more navigable. This idea was later taken up by Sir George Cayley, and eventually led to the development of dirigible balloons. Edgeworth also made a contribution of £50 towards the setting up of an Aeronautical Society in 1817, and his work helped to define the problems involved in designing a navigable balloon. Maria wrote an account of the Sadler ascent from Belvedere House in a letter to her mother:

Thursday morning, to our inexpressible joy, was fine and the flag, the signal that Sadler would ascend, was, to the joy of thousands, flying from the top of Nelson's Pillar. Dressed quickly – breakfasted I don't know how – job the coach was punctual: crowds in motion even at nine o'clock in the streets: tide flowing all one way to Belvidere gardens, lent by the proprietor for the occasion ... When we came near Belvidere, such strings of carriages, such crowds of people on the road and on the raised footpath, there was no stirring: troops lined the roads at each side; guard with officers at each entrance to prevent mischief; but unfortunately there were only two entrances, not nearly enough for such a confluence of people ...

Music and the most festive scene in the gardens: the balloon, the beautiful many-coloured balloon, chiefly maroon colour, with painted eagles and garlands, and arms of Ireland, hung under the trees, and filling fast from pipes and an apparatus which I leave for William's scientific description: terrace before Belvidere house – well-dressed groups parading on it, groups all over the gardens, mantles scarves and feathers floating: all the commonalty outside in fields at half price ... Soon we made our way behind the heels of the troopers' horses, who guarded a sacred circle around the balloon ...

The drum beats! The flag flies! Balloon full! It is moved from under the trees over the heads of the crowds: the car very light and slight – Mr. Sadler's son, a young lad, in the car. How the horses stood the motion of this vast body close to them, I can't imagine, but they did. The boy got out. Mr Sadler, quite composed, this being his twenty-sixth aerial ascent, got into his car: a lady, the duchess of Richmond I believe, presented to him a pretty flag. The balloon gave two majestic nods from side to side as the cords were cut. Whether the music continued at this moment to play or not, nobody could tell. No one spoke while the balloon successfully rose, rapidly cleared the trees and floated above our heads: loud shouts and huzzas, one man close to us exclaiming as he clasped his hands 'Ah musha, musha, God bless you! God be wid you!' Mr. Sadler, waving his flag and his hat and bowing to the world below, soon pierced a white cloud and disappeared; then emerging, the balloon looked like a moon, black on one side, silver on the other, then like a dark bubble; then less and less, and now only a speck is seen; and now a fleeting rack obscures it.

Soon after take-off, Sadler noticed a tear in the fabric, through which the gas was leaking and he climbed up to repair it using his neckcloth, but otherwise everything went smoothly. A south-westerly wind took him over the south coast of the Isle of Man, and he soon sighted Anglesey and flew over it. If he had chosen to land, he would have achieved his main aim. However, he wished to prove a theory he held about the existence of air currents at different altitudes, and was determined to end his journey in Liverpool as planned, so he continued on. He was over-confident about his ability to manoeuvre the balloon, and although at 4.30p.m. he was still on course for Liverpool, he was then driven out to sea again. He eventually had to come down in the sea. Incredibly, two nearby ships either failed to see him or refused to come to his aid; he then accomplished the extremely difficult task of ascending from the sea, as Crosbie had at first hoped to do in July 1785. Sadler was obliged to come down in the sea again at about 6p.m. and was rescued by a herring trawler, the *Victory*, which speared the balloon with its bowsprit. He had crossed the Irish Sea as far as Anglesey, and had covered a total of 280 miles, 237 of them over water. However, he had not made landfall, so the attempt was technically a failure.

Sadler soon published an account of the event, as this was by then a standard way for balloonists to make some profit from their adventures. This extract is from his journal:

> Beneath me lay stretched the city of Dublin with its suburbs skirting the bay, which lie a burnished mirror reflecting the beams of the sun exhibited a blaze of lustre too dazzling for the eye to rest upon – a grove of masts marked the course of the river and the passing vessels animated by their swelling sails the richness of the scene. From my elevated situation I was not only enabled to penetrate into the recesses of the Wicklow mountains but to overlook their ridges and bring within the field of vision the distant ocean and the blue horizon here and there broken by a sail – in a word, the country to the south and west of Dublin, interspersed with villages and fields, the amphitheatre of hills and mountains, the broad expanse of ocean, the bay, the small breakers beating on the islands and the rocky shore, the sails and vessels glancing in the sun; all combined presented a prospect which fancy may contemplate but words can give no adequate idea of and to enjoy which was in itself a reward for any hazard that might attend my undertaking.

A general election was about to be held at the time, and a satirical piece in the style of reporting used by the aeronauts was published, making some interesting topical points:

BALLOON.

AN

AUTHENTIC NARRATIVE,

OF

The Ærial Voyage,

OF

MR. SADLER,

ACROSS THE IRISH CHANNEL,

FROM

Belvedere-House, Drumcondra;

IN THE NEIGHBOURHOOD OF

DUBLIN,

On THURSDAY, OCTOBER 1st, 1812;

With some observations on the important objects connected with

ÆROSTATION.

TO WHICH IS ANNEXED,

A CHART OF THE CHANNEL,

Shewing his Course and place of Descent.

SOLD FOR THE BENEFIT OF MR. SADLER,

And Printed by W. H. Tyrrell, No. 17, *College-Green, Dublin.*

1812.

Title page of James Sadler's account of his flight of 1812. (Courtesy of National Library of Ireland.)

After throwing out three rheams of the *Hibernian Journal* which I had taken up as ballast, rose into the current of Election promises, very strong and oppressive – felt nearly stifled ... Met with several Castles in the Air; one occupied by a projector who meditated the payment of the National Debt; he had a large spunge tied to his girdle but I was moving too rapidly to ask him what he was going to do with it ...

At this period opened the valve, and descended nearer the Earth; had a bow from Public Opinion and the Liberty of the Press who were running as fast as they could into the upper regions, from a grim fellow called Ex Officio; they mentioned their intention of rusticating for some time in the suburbs of Elysium, where they expected, after next term, to be joined by their old friends, Trial by Jury and Habeas Corpus.

I now threw out a great deal of sand which I am since sorry to hear, fell into the eyes of many of the members of the Corporation of Dublin, whom Mr. G. even before they had been totally blinded, had long been in the habit of leading by the nose, and mounted quite out of sight of the world into the clear atmosphere of common sense. There I saw wonderful things – the futility of protracted war, and the necessity of REFORM and EMANCIPATION recorded in large capitals; I peeped through a micro-scope at Lord Castlereagh's talents but could discover nothing though the highest power was applied. I had a complete view of all the benefits to be derived from conciliation and procured a bucket of the water of oblivion to put out the Orange fire and promote harmony ...

One of James Sadler's sons, (William) Windham Sadler, made his first flight at the age of seventeen. Some sources state that Windham was born near Dublin, but the *Oxford Dictionary of National Biography* gives Pimlico, London as his birthplace. Windham made some successful balloon ascents in England in 1814; one was from Burlington House, London, accompanied by Mary Thompson, who was described as a friend of the Sadler family, and who may have been an actress; she was 'renowned in the Dramatic Corp,' according to J.E. Hodgson. This was her first ascent and she showed that she was as intrepid as her partner.

Assessing the conditions, she asked him, 'Can you go up?' 'Certainly,' came the reply. 'Then, what man dare, I dare,' she gamely responded. They travelled forty-eight miles at a rate of about a mile a minute and landed safely in Essex. The pair returned in triumph to London, followed by crowds along the Strand. Sadler made a solo ascent to mark the royal jubilee later that year. He was by profession a gas engineer, and had worked with the Liverpool Gas Company; for many of his adventures in England he was able to connect to town gas supplies, making the filling of the balloon much quicker and more reliable.

The Sadler family must have keenly felt the challenge of the Irish Sea crossing, because in 1816 they turned their attentions to Ireland again. Father and son worked together, but it seems that by this stage Windham was doing most of the flying. He set off from the square of the New Barracks in Cork in early September 1816, after the Countess of Shannon presented flags to him. He probably used the same balloon as had previously ascended from Burlington House, which was 75ft in diameter and capable of lifting (if not accommodating) seventy-two people. This journey took him as far as Robert's Cove; he sent his father a letter from Ringabella asking him to send some transport to Fountainstown, where the balloon was being kept.

In October 1816, a notice on the front page of the *Freeman's Journal* announced that another attempt would be made to cross the Irish Sea. It was headed with an image of the 1812 Sadler balloon in the sea, and the notice informed the public that the new balloon could be viewed at the Dublin Society premises in Hawkins Street. The flight took place from the square of Richmond Barracks in early November, and two men were on board: Windham Sadler and Edmond D. Livingston. They travelled for about thirty miles but in a completely opposite direction to the sea, finally coming down in the Bog of Allen. The area was very thinly populated, but they were led to a nearby cottage by the sound of a barking dog. Afterwards, the two men gave lectures on aerostation at Dublin Society House, and displayed some 'philosophical fireworks', all for an entrance charge of 2s 6d.

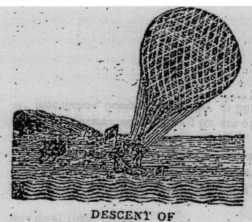

DESCENT OF

MR. SADLER,

In the Irish Channel,
After passing over 287 Miles of Water, and 43 by Land

MR. SADLER,

(Late Member of the Board of Naval Works, and
Inspector of Chemistry to the Army and Navy.)
Respectfully informs the Nobility, Gentry, and Public of
Dublin, and its Vicinity,
That he intends Ascending with his

BALLOON,

From this City, the time and place of which will be duly
announced.
To-morrow, WEDNESDAY, SEPT. 25, 1816,
The Magnificent

BALLOON AND SUPERB CAR,
Will be

EXHIBITED

At the Dublin Society House,
(HAWKINS'S STREET;)
The Members of which have, in the kindest and most liberal
manner, granted it for that purpose.
☞ BALLOONS are sent up in the Exhibition Room,
and to some of them Parachutes attached, which disengaging
themselves from the Balloons, shew the nature of a Descent
with a Parachute.
Admittance................1s. 8d.
Open every day from Eleven in the morning until dusk, for
a short time previous to the Ascent.

Advertisement for
Sadler's flight of
1816. (Courtesy of
National Library of
Ireland.)

The summer of 1817 saw a flurry of balloon activity, again with the Sadlers to the fore. James and Windham jointly planned another attempt at an Irish Sea crossing, with the son ultimately completing a solo flight. He specifically stated that his aim was 'to preserve to the family the honour of terminating an undertaking' and to win 'the undisputed palm of pre-eminence'. Newspaper notices said Sadler would ascend alone on 21 July, but that if the wind did not favour a channel cross- ing, there would be an alternative ascent by Mr Livingston and Miss Thompson at 2p.m. It seems that these two were working in associa- tion with the Sadlers and that the back-up plan was put in place to mitigate any disappointment among the spectators. There were some signs of friction however, as evidenced by a notice denying a rumour that Livingston had refused to fly with Sadler. The notice claimed, on the contrary, that Livingston was very keen to accompany Mr Sadler, but that it simply was not possible to accommodate two passengers, because of ballast requirements.

The Sadlers first approached the Dublin Society (which by then owned Leinster House) for permission to fly from there, but were refused. They were, however, again allowed to use the Society's Hawkins Street premises to display the balloon. The request to fly from Leinster House suggests that the Sadlers were well aware of Crosbie's earlier attempt from there, and that they wished to surpass it, although there is no specific mention of this. Arrangements were then made to set off from Portobello Barracks in Rathmines, in another parallel to the 1785 flight from Royal Barracks. Flags on the GPO (which was then in College Green) and on Nelson's Pillar were to signify to the public that the flight would proceed. On 22 July 1817, two pilot balloons were sent up at 11a.m. and 1p.m., and the day was deemed suitable for the crossing. Windham took off at 1.30p.m., having received flags from Lady Jane Loftus. According to the *Dublin Journal*, a crowd of 100,000 witnessed the ascent, but the vast majority watched from outside the Barracks, and once again, the takings did not cover the expenses. The car was made of wickerwork covered with glazed leather, and James

ÆROSTATION.

A NARRATIVE

OF

THE ÆRIAL VOYAGE

OF

MR. WINDHAM SADLER,

ACROSS THE

Irish Channel,

FROM PORTOBELLO BARRACKS,

IN THE NEIGHBOURHOOD OF

DUBLIN,

On TUESDAY, JULY 22d, 1817.

TO WHICH IS ANNEXED,

A CHART OF THE CHANNEL,

Shewing his Course and Place of Descent.

DUBLIN:

Printed by William Henry Tyrrell, No. 17, College-Green.

1817.

Title page of Windham Sadler's account of his flight across the Irish Sea, 1817. (Courtesy of National Library of Ireland.)

Sadler helped his son to attach the car to the balloon. The crowd's last view of Sadler was of him entering a dark cloud and raising a glass of wine to his lips. After an uneventful journey, he landed about a mile south of Holyhead at 7.05p.m. He was welcomed by local people, including Captain Skinner of the packet boat which sailed between Holyhead and Dublin, and they helped him to secure the balloon. While staying in Holyhead, he was reported as going several fathoms underwater in a diving bell.

When he returned to Dublin some days later, he and his father went to pay their respects to the Lord Lieutenant, as Richard Crosbie had done thirty-two years earlier. Despite so many echoes of the career of Crosbie, and despite the detailed accounts written by the Sadlers, neither mentions the pioneer of flight in Ireland. It seems churlish, and even out of character, and certainly contrasts with the graciousness shown by Charles and by Lunardi towards their predecessors. James Sadler, in particular, would have been well aware of Crosbie from the 1780s. Even the *Freeman's Journal* seems to have erased Crosbie's memory, and the only reference to him was by a letter writer, who had witnessed the flight of Richard McGwire in 1785. In recognition of the historic nature of the 1817 flight as the culmination of a long-standing ambition, and in confirmation that the flight had lost money, friends of the Sadlers some weeks later launched a fund to defray their expenses. The first subscribers were the Duke of Leinster, Lord Forbes, the Lord Mayor, Sheriffs Dixon and Reid, Lady Jane Loftus, and Col Pelly.

Both Sadlers made a strong case for the science of aerostation and appealed for more support for it. Windham regretted that ballooning had been mainly an experiment in profit and amusement, and that scientific research had not been to the fore:

> The element of air, pregnant with wonder and daily presenting to the eye of ever common observation matter of astonishment, alone remains comparatively unexplored and aerostation ... neglected and uncultivated.

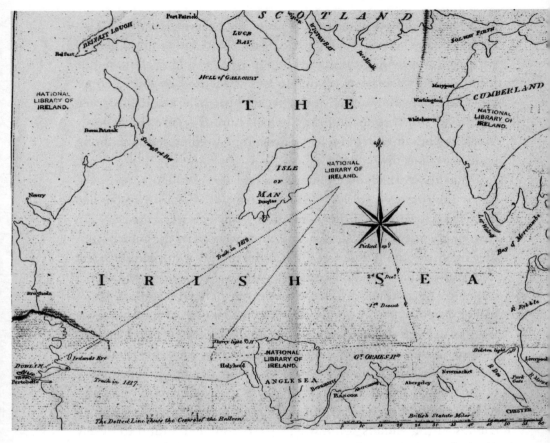

Tracks of the two Sadler flights, 1812 and 1817. (Courtesy of National Library of Ireland.)

There is a little more information on Livingston and Miss Thompson, who were involved in several flights with the Sadlers, although the relationship appears to have been fraught. Livingston (sometimes rendered as Livingstone or Levingston) was an Irishman, but I have not discovered any more information on his background, except that he had an address in Drumcondra in 1822. Mary Thompson became the first woman to make a balloon flight in Ireland, following Miss Durry's failure in 1786. A month after Sadler's triumph in crossing the Irish

Sea, he announced that his balloon would ascend with Livingston and Thompson on 18 August, and that when the balloon was a mile high, 'a parachute with an animal will be detached'. The notice also stated that a number of balloons would be sent up with 'moroons' or small fireworks. Increasingly, balloon flights were associated with novelties and since the first parachute descent had been made in Paris in 1797, these were often part of the entertainment, sometimes using animals. According to F.E. Dixon, the animal dropped by Mary Thompson was a tortoise.

On this occasion, however, James Sadler objected to Livingston's ascent, causing some confusion. Livingston felt obliged to keep to his advertised programme but right up to the day of the launch, Sadler continued to object. In the end, he agreed, but on condition that Livingston would descend as soon as Thompson requested him to. Privately, James Sadler instructed her not to allow Livingston to go over the Dublin hills. She carried out her instructions to the letter, and Livingston kept his word, so when she requested it, the balloon did descend, rapidly and dangerously, into Marlay Park, owned by Mr La Touche. Livingston wished to ascend again but Mary prevailed on him not to, saying it would offend Mr Sadler. There is insufficient detail in news reports to understand fully what was going on, but it may be that Sadler feared that Livingston might replicate the Irish Sea crossing and so take some of the gloss from Windham's achievement. Or perhaps he simply feared for the safety of Mary Thompson. In another echo of the Crosbie era, the *Freeman's Journal* deplored the delay and mismanagement of the whole affair, the time wasted by people in watching the show, and the fact that they had to stand on damp ground for hours. The paper regretted that on every occasion of a balloon flight, the town emptied into the country, and it alluded to a bizarre claim that 1,500 people had contracted a disease from standing around too long at a previous balloon event.

Livingston made two flights from Dublin in 1822, and the first showed that he had a generous and philanthropic nature. In 1821-22,

MR. SADLER

MOST respectfully informs the Nobility, Gentry, and Inhabitants of Dublin and its Vicinity, that his Balloon will make its
SECOND ASCENT
THIS DAY, AUGUST 18, 1817,
FROM
PORTOBELLO BARRACKS,
When MISS TOMPSON and MR. LIVINGSTON will Ascend, at Two o'Clock precisely.
And when the Balloon has attained the Altitude of a Mile, A PARACHUTE, with an Animal, will be detached.

The Gates of the Barrack will be opened for the Admission of Company, at Ten o'Clock.—The Process of Inflating will commence at Eleven, which will be announced by the Firing of a Gun.—A Second Gun will announce the Balloon being inflated.—A Third, the attaching the Car.—A Fourth, the Pilot-Balloon, to shew the direction of the large one.—A Fifth, THE ASCENT.

A Stage will be erected, from which the Balloon will Ascend, so that every person within the Barrack may have an uninterrupted View.

Admittance 2s. 6d.

Signals from Nelson's Pillar and the Post-Office will be made, if the Day be favourable for the Ascent;—should, however, the Wind blow in the direction of the Sea, or the Weather prove unfavourable, it will be postponed until the first suitable Day.

Previous to the Ascent, a number of BALLOONS will be sent up, with MOROONS attached to them.

Carriages, &c. will be Admitted by the Gate from Rathmines Road; that on the Canal will be opened for those on Foot.

☞ Tickets to be had at the Dublin Society-House; at 85, Marlborough-street; and at No. 17, College-green.

Advertisement for Livingston and Thompson flight, 1817. (Courtesy of National Library of Ireland.)

the potato crop failed in the south and west of the country, and there was famine. It is believed that over 100, 000 people died in what was a harbinger of the great famine. Many fundraising events were held to provide relief to the distressed. Livingston's flight was planned for June, and, on learning that a play and a ball held in Dublin as fundraisers for famine relief had yielded very little money, he announced that all profits from his flight would go to the Mansion House Committee's efforts to relieve distress. This committee was headed by the Lord Mayor. All Livingston requested in return was the assistance of some

Livingston's descent in the Irish Sea near Baldoyle, 1822. (Courtesy of Science Museum London.)

people to act as cashiers and stewards on the day. His noble gesture was hailed as a magnanimous act and Livingston was highly praised. He also announced that he would drop tickets for the state lottery from the basket as he ascended and that the finders would be able to claim prizes. These two features combined to make the launch a considerable success, and Livingston handed over £231 4s to the Lord Mayor. This was among the highest single amounts donated to the fund, and the launch must rank as possibly the only profitable one in Ireland up to then. It is to Livingston's great credit that the money went to a humanitarian cause, but the flight, alas, was not very successful. The balloon took off from Portobello Barracks, which was reported as presenting 'a very agreeable *coup d'oeil*'. All seemed to go well at first, with the balloon 'in a direct line for Holyhead', but it was then seen to be driven northward. It ultimately came down in the Irish Sea, close to the shore near Baldoyle.

Livingston was warmly encouraged by the Lord Mayor and others to hold a second flight for his own profit, and he agreed to do so. This flight took place in August, again from Portobello Barracks. An incident at the launch provided great amusement to the waiting crowd. A platform had been erected as a viewing-point and it was commandeered by a group of dandies who proceeded to make an exhibition of themselves. But 'some envious elf' went underneath and removed supports from the platform which then toppled to the ground. 'Suddenly they became a promiscuous heap, moving on all fours, to the great injury of stays and derangement of well-adjusted stiffners. It afforded great amusement to many who diverted themselves by enjoying a laugh at the expense of a set of coxcombs.'

Livingston took off at 2.40p.m. and was seen gliding over Ranelagh and Cullenswood, reaching Stillorgan at 3p.m. However, the balloon this time fell to earth in an area described as 'Corner's Court, Cabinteely' (today's Cornelscourt). There, Livingston was attacked by farmers who claimed he had destroyed their crops, and who demanded compensation with menaces. They held on to the balloon and to the balloonist, until he finally handed over £5. The Horse Police were sent for, but by the time they arrived Livingston was safe in the house of Counsellor Patten. The *Freeman's Journal* lamented this attack by the peasantry on a man who had so generously supported their suffering brethren in the south of Ireland.

To add to his woes, Livingston learned that this second flight was not a financial success. The *Freeman's Journal's* comment was terse, 'Mr Livingston's losses last Monday and today's expenses will greatly exceed £200. We know it is only necessary to state this fact. We are, therefore, done.' This rebuke must have had some effect, because his total loss was later said to have been £90. Livingston was next reported as ascending from Preston, where he suffered a broken leg and other injuries when he was thrown out of the car from a height of 15ft. In June 1824, he was back in Ireland, being castigated for a failed attempt from Belfast, showing that little had changed in that respect since 1785. A Belfast paper declared, 'It is highly culpable to sport with the patience of 40,000 people, and it not only brings discredit on the individual doing so, but it prevents those who have been duped again coming forward to encourage similar undertakings.' Nonetheless, Livingston managed to redeem himself by successfully ascending a few days later, and the tone of reports was more favourable. Once again, there are echoes of Crosbie's experience with the press, and also of his thwarted effort to fly from Belfast in 1786.

The toll of lives lost in the early years of ballooning was high. Jean Pierre Blanchard suffered a heart attack in 1808 and died while attempting a parachute jump in 1809; his young wife, Sophie, met her death in a truly horrific accident in 1819, when her balloon was ignited by fireworks in a display in Tivoli Gardens, London. She fell first on to the roof of a building, and then to the ground. The ever-present dangers of this new enterprise of ballooning had been brought home to people at an early stage with the death of Pilatre de Rozier in June 1785, as he attempted to cross the Channel in a combined hydrogen and hot-air balloon. He and his companion plunged to earth when the balloon exploded at about 5,000ft. So, the first man to fly became the first to die in an air disaster. Another of the intrepid early aeronauts was an Italian named Count Zambeccari, who died in 1812 when his combination balloon burst into flames near Bologne. Vincent Lunardi is believed to have died in poverty in Portugal in 1806.

The year 1824 saw several ballooning tragedies. On 25 May, Thomas Harris lost his life in a balloon crash-landing near Croydon. His companion, an eighteen-year-old named Jane Stocks, survived the trauma. Harris was conducting an experiment in landing technique, and it is thought likely that when he realised that the balloon was descending

Contemporary illustration of the death of Pilatre de Rozier and companion over the Channel, 1785.
(Courtesy of Princeton University Press.)

too rapidly, he threw himself out to lighten it, in order to save Jane's life. Young Windham Sadler continued to make balloon ascents, including one from his father's native Oxford in the early summer of 1824, but in September, he met a tragic end on his thirty-first flight, near Blackburn. He was hanging by the leg from the basket for a short time but then fell to his death. He was only twenty-seven years old. His distraught father never flew again, and died in 1828. Surprisingly, amid all the balloon-related news reports of 1824, there were no substantial references to the death of Richard Crosbie, which occurred on 30 May, although there would have been an obvious link to the other stories.

These events of 1824, and particularly Crosbie's death, make it an appropriate year with which to end this story. I have not traced any further flights by Edmond Livingston. The achievements of these two intrepid Irish balloonists, one a true pioneer and the other a worthy successor, who dared to believe in their own prowess and to commit their lives to the fragile vessels of the air, deserve belated recognition. They survived their exploits, more or less unscathed, and at the very least, succeeded in making their fellow citizens more air-minded. They lifted the heads and hearts of Irishmen and Irishwomen on many memorable occasions, and held them spellbound and mesmerised. Their achievements are equally worthy of our admiration today.

The common-sense attitude to ballooning was succinctly captured by G.A. Sala, quoted by Hodgson, whose only flight ended in a crash landing in 1851:

> It is madness and folly to permit any enthusiast or charlatan who may be in the possession of a silk bag which he can afford to fill with coal-gas, to risk his own life among the clouds, as well as those of the madcaps who are with him, for the amusement of some hundreds of gobemouches who have paid a shilling a head to see their fellow creatures commit constructive suicide.

Fortunately, there will always be enthusiasts and madcaps (aka geniuses) such as Richard Crosbie who are inspired not by common sense and security but by 'a lonely impulse of delight' of which W.B. Yeats wrote in his poem 'An Irish Airman Foresees His Death'.

❦ 12 ❦

ENVOI

*There's something in a flying horse
There's something in a huge balloon ...*

'Peter Bell, Prologue' (1798), William Wordsworth

There has always been much discussion with regard to the practical benefits of ballooning, and the question posed to Benjamin Franklin, 'Of what use are these machines?' still challenges. Richard Holmes cites several ways in which ballooning produced practical results. There were benefits in relation to astronomy, for example, and the early suggestion of using balloons as observation platforms for telescopes has been linked to the ultimate development of the orbiting Hubble telescope in 1997. As Crosbie found over the Shannon estuary, aerial views gave a revealing perspective on the physical world, the course of rivers and the relationship between town and country. The establishment of the British Ordnance Survey was partly influenced by ballooning. The new sciences of meteorology and astronomy, the development of theories of atmospheric pressure, cloud classification, and the establishment of wind-scale systems can also be linked to ballooning.

Holmes makes this fascinating observation on the phenomenon of public displays which accompanied balloon events:

> Ballooning proved to have extraordinary theatrical power to attract crowds, embody longing, and mix terror and the sublime with farce. It became showmanship, carnival, pure euphoria. A successful balloon launch, in the hands of one of the early masters like Pilatre, Lunardi or Blanchard, became a communal expression of hope and wonder, of courage and comedy. The balloon crowd (especially in Paris) foreshadowed another kind of crowd – the revolutionary crowd. It contained elements of prophecy, both political and scientific. It was like a collective gasp of hope and longing.

Thomas Carlyle, in *The French Revolution*, wrote:

> Beautiful invention; mounting heavenward, so beautifully – so unguidably! Emblem of much and of our Age of Hope itself.

It seems to me that for Richard Crosbie, the sheer simple delight of soaring high above the world was an end in itself. He was motivated by patriotism and by fame, but he so clearly relished the magic and the thrill that it does not seem to matter so much that he did not achieve his ultimate aim. The experience of ecstacy, or *ex-stasis*, standing outside oneself, was what he sought and achieved. He helped to lift people's eyes and hearts sky-wards, and open up their imaginations to limitless possibilities. The balloon was, and still is, a symbol of transcendence, of the possibility of rising above the mundane and the everyday, the petty concerns and intrigues of daily life. Crosbie had the soul of a poet, and he clearly exulted in the spirit-lift of his flights.

Wordsworth, Coleridge, and other Romantic poets were fascinated by ballooning, which has always symbolised the soaring human spirit in some way. The idealistic Percy Bysshe Shelley was an enthusiast, and a keen follower of Sadler's experiments. In Oxford in 1811, just before he was expelled for expressing atheistic views, Shelley had this vision for Africa:

> Why are we so ignorant of the interior of Africa? – Why do we not dispatch intrepid aeronauts to cross it in every direction, and to survey the whole peninsula in a few weeks? The shadow of the first balloon, which a vertical sun would project precisely underneath it, as it glided over that hitherto unhappy country, would virtually emancipate every slave, and would annihilate slavery forever.

In 1812, shortly after a visit to Ireland, Shelley stood on a beach in Lynmouth, Devon, sending up a series of silk fire-balloons which had been sewn by his young wife Harriet. Each carried copies of his revolutionary pamphlet 'A Declaration of Rights'. He wrote a sonnet entitled 'To a Balloon, Laden with Knowledge', which began:

> Bright ball of flame that thro the gloom of even
> Silently takes thine ethereal way ...

In the early days, balloons were often dismissed as mere toys, baubles and playthings. Nowadays they are indeed playthings, an experience offered to tourists in scenic places, and they provide a unique sense of liberation and tranquility as they soar over the Serengeti or the Kalahari, or even the Boyne Valley. Ballooning is still a rare and treasured experience with only a small number of people ever having had the exhilaration of a flight. The ultimate ballooning achievement was a solo non-stop round-the-world flight by Steve Fossett in 2002.

Some things have not changed: at the 225th anniversary celebration of Crosbie's flight in Ranelagh in January 2010, I heard from the intrepid balloonist Tom McCormack that there is still no way of knowing where a flight might end, just as was the case with the early balloonists. Tom also told me that a balloon landing can be akin to a controlled crash, and I was reminded of Crosbie's achievement in effecting two safe landings on *terra firma* and one descent in the ocean.

The search for dirigibility or the power of controlling the balloon, which pre-occupied Richard Crosbie in 1784-85, and to which he made a distinctive contribution, proved a long search. Balloon and airship developments in the nineteenth century culminated in the invention of the Zeppelin in 1900, and the twentieth century brought a new era of heavier-than-air flight. But the balloon still retained a tremendous romantic appeal. As L.T.C. Rolt expressed it:

Commemoration of Crosbie's flight in Ranelagh Gardens in January 2010. (P.D. Lynch.)

George Cruickshank ,'Taxi Balloons'. (Courtesy of the Board of Trinity College Dublin.)

Only the balloon, a frail bladder of gas, unguidable, beautiful, comical, tragically ephemeral, a spherical microcosm of the great globe itself, affords man an aerial platform upon which he may stand, staring down in silence upon the mystery of his turning world.

Comparisons have inevitably been made between the first balloonists and the first astronauts of the mid-twentieth century, and it is true that experiments in sending up small animals were repeated in the early days of space exploration, as in 1957, when the dog Laika was launched into an orbit of the earth and died some hours into the flight. However, for me, the balloonists of the 1780s had more in common with the astonishing artist of the high-wire, Philippe Petit, whose exploits in walking a tightrope between the Twin Towers of the World Trade Centre in New York in 1974 enthralled and appalled spectators in equal measure.

The crowds who gathered in Manhattan to gaze in amazement at the 'man on wire' were prefigured by the crowd in a Manhattan without skyscrapers in 1800, watching Richard Crosbie's balloon, while he contemplated a manned flight.

Crosbie and Petit performed above the ground with only the slightest of materials preventing them from falling to their deaths – for one, the wire, and for the other, insubstantial materials of silk and wicker. They put their lives at extreme risk for the sake of their dreams. Both were entertainers, even stuntmen, but more besides, and both had made meticulous and successful plans in advance of their exploits. They relished the freedom and sheer exhilaration of stepping above the mundane, in an activity of no immediate purpose, although Petit's walks held a greater element of risk.

Photo by Tom McCormack.

Ranelagh Arts Festival celebration of the 225th anniversary of Richard Crosbie's flight. (Paragon Design, Ranelagh).

Crosbie and Petit were kindred spirits in another sense: they were artists in the medium of air. The novelist Paul Auster has written about the art of the high-wire walker, in terms which I believe are applicable to the art of the early balloonist:

> No art, it seems to me, so clearly emphasizes the deep aesthetic impulse inside us all. Each time we see a man walk on the wire, a part of us is up there with him. Unlike performances in other arts, the experience of the high wire is direct, unmediated, simple, and it requires no explanation whatsoever. The art is the thing itself, a life in its most naked delineation. And if there is beauty in this it is because of the beauty we feel inside ourselves.

Auster addresses the question of why Petit did his high-wire walk in New York and answers, 'For no other reason, I believe, than to dazzle the world with what he could do.' Richard Crosbie shared the same motivation, to dazzle his world. He succeeded brilliantly.

CROSBIE FAMILY HISTORY

The Crosbie family's origins were in Co. Laois, originally as a branch of the O'Mores, the senior and most powerful of the Seven Septs of Laois. The information here comes from Burke's *Irish Family Records*. They took the name McCrossan (*Mac an Chrosain*, the son of the rhymer) as the family held the hereditary Gaelic office of Chief Bard to the O'Mores. In the Tudor period, a McCrossan Chief Bard married an O'Kelly woman and they had two sons, Patrick and John. Both of these anglicised their names to Crosbie in around 1583, and John became a Protestant clergyman. He was appointed Bishop of Ardfert in December 1601 by Queen Elizabeth. He married Winifred O'Lalor, from another of the Seven Septs of Laois, and their eldest son, Walter, returned to the midlands, residing at Maryborough, now Portlaoise. He was created 1st Baronet in 1630. It is from Walter's line that the Wicklow branch is traced.

Walter's son John, 2nd Baronet, settled at Ballyfin, Co. Laois, and Warren, 3rd Baronet, lived at Crosbie Park, near Baltinglass, Co. Wicklow. He was a captain in the army and had served under the Duke of Marlborough in all his campaigns. He was granted a pension of £200 a year in 1727, and is said to have refused a peerage. Richard was born

Ballyheigue Castle today.

Ardfert Abbey in the
nineteenth century.

c.1756, as second son of Sir Paul Crosbie, 4th Baronet, and great-great-
great-great-grandson of John of Ardfert. There is no evidence of any
significant interaction between the Wicklow branch and their distant
relatives in Kerry in the late 1700s.

David, the second son of Bishop John, remained in Ardfert and from
him that line is traced. The Ardfert line reached the zenith of its social
status when William, 2nd Baron Branden [sic], 1st Viscount Crosbie, was created 1st Earl of Glandore in 1776. He married the daughter of the Earl of
Darnley. In 1777, his son John, 2nd Earl, married the society beauty Diana
Sackville, in a ceremony performed by the Archbishop of Canterbury at
her father's home in London. When he died without an heir in 1815, the
title became extinct. The succession of the Ardfert family from then on
was through the female line, and their name became Talbot-Crosbie.

The adjoining parish of Ballyheigue became another Crosbie strong-hold in the 1700s. The Ballyheigue branch of the Crosbies earned great notoriety in the early 1730s when they were implicated in the robbery of a cargo of silver bullion from a ship of the Danish East India Company which ran aground in Ballyheigue bay. The ensuing inquiry became an international incident and *cause célèbre* involving the authorities in London, Dublin and Copenhagen. After 300 years of prominence, the Ardfert and Ballyheigue branches sold their estates in the early 1920s, and there are no representatives of the Crosbie families living in the county today.

SIR EDWARD CROSBIE

The balloonist's older brother, Edward, 5th Baronet, was born c.1755, and was called to the Bar in 1778. He had a town house in Park Street, Dublin, and in 1786 was listed in Watson's *Almanack* as one of only five Baronets of Nova Scotia resident in Ireland. He lost his life during the Rebellion of 1798, in shocking circumstances: he was executed after the United Irishmen attacked Carlow town. Although he might be expected to reside in the Crosbie family home in Co. Wicklow, it was at his house at Viewmount on Browne's Hill, outside Carlow, that he was apprehended on the 24 May 1798. He was summarily tried by court martial, and hanged on 5 June. He was then beheaded and the severed head was placed on a pike outside Carlow jail, visible from his house, where his widow, Lady Castiliana, resided. No clergyman could be found to give him a proper burial and he was interred in the garden of his house. It was to be twelve months before he received a proper Christian burial, and two years before the full story of his trial was uncovered by his widow. It was an ignominious end for a prominent and widely respected man, who had acted as aide-de-camp to Henry Grattan in a review of the Volunteers in 1781. He had also been barrack master at Bray, Co. Wicklow.

Sir Edward Crosbie was only one of many who died in Carlow at this time of rebellion – some accounts have five hundred rebels killed in the attack on the town barracks – but there is a good deal of information on this particular death. The circumstances of his arrest and trial, and the subsequent difficulty in obtaining information from the authorities, drove his widow and relatives to publish a pamphlet with their account of what happened. They vehemently denied claims that he was a United Irishman, a deist or a republican, and asserted their belief that he had 'fallen sacrifice to ill-founded prejudice during an ungovernable paroxysm of party rage'. Crosbie's steward, Thomas Myler, was a leader of the United Irishmen in Carlow and deeply involved in the rebellion. It was his habit to dress in a green jacket, very similar to his master's, when he organised the rebels and addressed them. It suited Myler's purposes that his followers should believe that the master of Viewmount House was aiding their cause. Myler addressed a group of United Irishmen outside the walls of Crosbie's estate on the night of 24 May 1798, and some may have had the impression that the figure addressing them was Crosbie. The next day, the group marched into Carlow, attacked the barracks, and was routed. Later in the day, a party of military under Col Mahon arrived at Crosbie's house, and arrested him.

Lady Castiliana believed the detention would be temporary and asked for twenty-four hours notice of any trial. She tried to find a defence lawyer in Carlow, but failed. When she later visited her husband in Carlow jail, she was told the trial would begin in just one hour. Edward Crosbie was charged with aiding and abetting a conspiracy, and Major Dennis of Mountmellick presided at the court martial. With so little time to arrange counsel and a defence, Crosbie was convicted on evidence provided by his butler and some of his servants. A fellow prisoner, William Farrell, years later gave an account of Crosbie's demeanour in jail in the hours before his death, which adds some telling details to the story. He described Crosbie as a man who lived a retired life, and who was kind and affable to those of lower rank in society. He was not 'one of those fawning sycophants that could stoop to any meanness or any oppression of the poor or any plunder of the public'. One of his last acts in prison was to ask tradesmen and shopkeepers to send their accounts for settling, indicating that he must have foreseen his end. 'It was a sad and gloomy evening for all the prisoners,' wrote William Farrell, 'for we all very naturally concluded that, where such a gentleman as Sir Edward Crosbie got such usage, the chance of those in the humbler walks of life must have been very precarious indeed.' Farrell was fortunate to be one of the survivors.

Some features of the trial only emerged after dogged pursuit of the authorities by Lady Castiliana. Evidence cited against Crosbie was varied. In an act of generosity, he had sent money to aid starving prisoners in Carlow jail the previous February, and this humanitarian gesture was read as support for the rebels. It was also rumoured that Lord Edward Fitzgerald had visited Crosbie at his home in Carlow. Crosbie denied this, saying he had only ever seen Fitzgerald once, from a distance.

The most serious charge was that Crosbie had prior knowledge of what was about to happen in Carlow on 24 May. This was true; Crosbie had planned to go to the town, but was dissuaded when a servant warned him against going on that day. Crosbie knew that something was afoot, but by this time regarded himself as a virtual prisoner in his home, unable to alert the authorities. Crosbie was shown the pikes assembled by Myler and his men on the night before the attack, and could not have been in any doubt about their function. In his own evidence, Crosbie admitted that he knew on the 24 May that an attack was planned, but felt powerless to prevent it. He regretted that he had not done more to dissuade his servants. He anticipated his end, saying, 'I fear I shall fall victim to the madness of the times.'

It seems that the reason for Crosbie's execution was that he had incurred some local resentment, probably related to a duel with a young local man from a prominent and powerful family. According to Farrell, the man was a Counsellor Burton, who fired first and missed, while Crosbie then graciously declined to fire. Lady Castiliana also established that the servants who testified against Crosbie had been tortured and threatened, and that favourable witnesses were prevented from giving evidence. There is no doubt that Crosbie was an innocent victim and that a miscarriage of justice led to his death. His wife was shunned and isolated locally by neighbours who were 'intimidated, inimical or prejudiced,' and she was denied access to the proceedings of the court martial. On applying to the Lord Lieutenant, Cornwallis, she eventually received the reply that the records could not be found. Undergoing harassment from the local militia, Lady Castiliana fled to England, 'with a distracted mind and a bleeding heart'.

Two years later, she secured a copy of the court martial, on condition that no further prosecution would be taken. The pamphlet was written to refute the evidence presented at the court martial. Lady Castiliana was a formidable woman, and a tenacious defender of her husband's reputation. Farrell admired her strenuous defence of her husband, and described her as 'an honour to her sex'. She was daughter of Warren Westenra, MP, of Roscommon and was widow of Capt. Henry Dod when she married Crosbie. I have found no records of any involvement by Richard in the family's strenuous efforts to clear Edward's name. He seems to have been, to all intents and purposes, dead to his family and former life while he was abroad, and it is not possible to say how much he knew of events in Ireland. The prolific author Turtle Bunbury has more information on Viewmount House and on the Crosbie family on his website www.turtlebunbury.com/history.

THE CROSBIE SUCCESSION

John Crosbie, Bishop of Ardfert m. Winifred O'Lalor, Co. Laois.

|

Walter, 1st Baronet, m. Mabel Browne, of Totteridge, Herts. and Molahiffe and Rosse, Co. Kerry.

|

John, 2nd Baronet, Ballyfin, Co. Laois, m. Ellice Fitzgerald, Walterstown, Co. Kildare

|

Maurice of Knockmoy, Co. Laois (attainted 1688), m. Dorothea Annesley, Ballysonan, Co. Kildare

|

Warren, 3rd Baronet, Crosbie Park, m. Dorothy Howard, Haverares, Northumberland

|

Paul, 4th Baronet, m. Mary Daniel, Frodsham, Cheshire

|

Edward, 5th Baronet, barrister, m. Castiliana Dod, (widow of Capt. Henry Dod), *née* Westenra of Rossmore Park, Co. Monaghan

|

William, 6th Baronet, army officer, m. Dorothea Walsh, Dublin.

Sir William, 6th Baronet, was severely wounded at the battle of Bergen-op-Zoom. As he died without an heir, the title passed to William Richard, grandson of Richard Crosbie, the balloonist. Sir William died in 1860 and was buried in the churchyard of St Paul's church in Bray, Co. Wicklow. His wife, Dorothea, was buried there in 1880, and his unmarried sister Henrietta in 1857. Also buried there are Henrietta Walsh, daughter of Sir Paul Crosbie, who died in 1828, and her son Henry, who died in 1847.

FAMILY OF RICHARD CROSBIE

According to Burke's *Irish Family Records* (1976), Richard Crosbie married Charlotte, the only daughter of Archibald Armstrong, of Twickenham, Middlesex and Rosina, King's County. The wedding took place in December 1780. It is likely that Middlesex is an error, as there was a house called Twickenham near Ballycumber, Co. Offaly, which was the seat of the Armstrong family. (There is at least one mistake in Burke's genealogy, where he describes Edward Crosbie as an 'eminent balloonist' instead of his brother Richard.) There is further information on Charlotte's background in another publication, Burke's *General and Heraldic History of the Commoners of Great Britain and Ireland* (1838), which traces her descent from the Armstrong line of Garry Castle House, King's County (Co. Offaly). It says that her father, Archibald Armstrong, was born at Barnagrotty in 1726, married Margaret Bagot of Ard, King's County, and died on 13 June 1793, leaving a son Andrew and a daughter Charlotte Margaret. Archibald's father was Andrew, who was treasurer of King's County and for some time the comptroller of the household of the Lord Lieutenant.

Crosbie relatives with Councillor Mary Freehill at the unveiling of Rory Breslin's statue of Richard Crosbie in Ranelagh Gardens, 2008. (Daragh Owens).

Richard and his wife Charlotte had at least one son, Edward, of Dublin, who became an army officer. He married Jane Henry of Co. Kildare, and died on 25 June 1834, ten years after his father. He left a son William Richard, who inherited the title of 7th Baronet when his cousin, the 6th Baronet, died without an heir. His son William Edward, 8th Baronet, died in 1877 without a male heir. Burke does not list any other children of Richard and Charlotte, but it is clear that they also had a daughter, who, according to the *Masonic Review* account cited in Chapter 10, became a novelist. Her name may have been Mary.

Richard Crosbie has direct descendants living in England today, and other relatives living in Ireland. In December 2009, I had the pleasure of meeting the great-great-great-great granddaughter of the celebrated balloonist in London.

★★★

Richard Crosbie, second son of Sir Paul Crosbie of Crosbie Park, m. Charlotte Armstrong, of Co. Offaly.

|

Edward, of Dublin, army officer, m. Jane Henry, Co. Kildare

|

William Richard, 7th Baronet, of Latrobe Cottage, Bedford, m. Catherine Madden, Co. Kilkenny.

|

William Edward Douglas, 8th and last Baronet, m. Georgina Marsh, Bath

|

Marjorie (born 1895) m. (1920) Godfrey Sutcliffe Marsh, London.

TIMELINE

*c.*1756:   Richard Crosbie born in Crosbie Park, Co. Wicklow.

1773:   Crosbie enters Trinity College. Reported as first conceiving of human flight.

1779:   Alleged attack on brothel of Peg Plunket/Mrs Leeson.

1780:   December: Marriage of Richard Crosbie and Charlotte Armstrong.

1783   5 June: Montgolfier brothers launch first hot-air balloon in Annonay.

27 August: First hydrogen balloon in Paris.

19 September: Animals in flight at Versailles.

20 November: First manned hot-air balloon flight by de Rozier and d'Arlandes in Paris.

1 December: First manned hydrogen balloon flight by Charles and Robert in Paris.

1784   4 February: Riddick sends up a balloon from Marlborough Green, Dublin.

7 February: Crosbie announces his intention of constructing an aerial chariot for purpose of a manned flight.

April: Crosbie displays model to Trinity fellows.

13 April: Crosbie appeals to Lord Charlemont for support.

4 June: In Paris, Madame Thible makes first flight by a woman.

25 August: Tytler's ascent in Edinburgh: first manned flight in Britain.

15 September: Lunardi's first flight in England.

16 August: Crosbie displays aeronautical chariot in Ranelagh Gardens.

6 September: Balloon with cat sent up from Ranelagh.

21 September: Dinwiddie lecture in Dublin.

2 October: Duchess of Rutland releases balloon from Ranelagh.

4 October: Sadler, the first English airman, ascends from Oxford.

25 December: Crosbie's proposed flight deferred.

1785   4 January: Crosbie's attempted flight from Ranelagh Gardens fails.

7 January: Blanchard and Jeffries cross the English Channel.

19 January: Crosbie's successful flight from Ranelagh Gardens.

10 May: Crosbie's attempt from Royal Barracks fails.

12 May: McGwire succeeds in flying from Royal Barracks and comes down in Irish Sea.

15 June: Pilatre de Rozier and companion are killed in attempt to cross English Channel.

17 June: Dr Potain's flight from Dublin

29 June: First flight in England by a woman, Mrs Sage.

19 July: Crosbie's successful flight from Leinster Lawn.

October: Crosbie plans another flight from Dublin, which does not take place.

1786   2 January: First date mooted for Limerick flight.

27 April: Crosbie's longest flight, from Limerick along the Shannon estuary and into Clare.

18 April: Durry brother and sister attempted flight from Ranelagh Gardens.

May/June: Lunardi visits Dublin but makes no flight.

May: Crosbie's proposes Belfast flight to Lord Charlemont.

1793   9 January: Blanchard makes first balloon flight in the United States.

28 December: Crosbie makes first appearance on US stage.

1797   Crosbie benefit performance of *The Poor Soldier* in St John's Theatre, New York.

1798   5 June: Sir Edward Crosbie executed in Carlow.

1800   3 October: First reference to Crosbie's lectures on aerostation in New York.

27 October: Crosbie's balloon experiment in Mount Vernon Garden, New York.

Winter: Crosbie plans a manned flight from New York, which does not take place.

1812   1 October: James Sadler's flight from Belvedere House. Crosses over Anglesey, but comes down in sea.

1816   Windham Sadler's flight in Cork.

1817   22 July: Windham Sadler makes first successful crossing of the Irish Sea.

        18 August: Mary Thompson becomes the first woman to make a flight in Ireland, with Livingston.

1819   Winter: Crosbie is discovered living in poverty in Baltimore, Maryland.

1820   Spring: Crosbie returns to Dublin.

1822   27 June: Livingston's flight from Portobello Barracks ends in Irish Sea.

        5 August: Livingston's flight from Portobello Barracks ends in Cornelscourt.

1824   25 May: Thomas Harris killed in balloon accident in Croydon.

        30 May: Richard Crosbie dies in Dublin.

        9 June: Livingston ascends in Belfast at second attempt.

        29 September: Windham Sadler killed in balloon accident near Blackburn.

1828   26 March: James Sadler dies in Oxford.

ACKNOWLEDGEMENTS

Most of the research for this book has involved consulting microfilms of old newspapers in the National Library of Ireland and in Dublin City Library and Archive. I have also consulted sources in Trinity College Library (Department of Early Printed Books), The British Library, the Library of the Royal Irish Academy, the Library of the Freemason Grand Lodge of Ireland, and Dún Laoghaire-Rathdown County Libraries. My thanks to the staff of all these libraries for their unfailing courtesy and assistance.

A special word of gratitude to Ms Laura Ruttum in the Milstein Division of United States History, Local History and Genealogy at the New York Public Library, for providing me with copies of newspaper articles on Crosbie's balloon experiments in New York, and for patiently dealing with my numerous follow-up questions. I also wish to express my gratitude to Ms Rayanne Byatt of Coventry Heritage and Arts Trust Library and to the staff of the Library of the University of Michigan. I also received assistance from Bibliothèque Nationale de France and from the library of the Royal Aeronautical Society.

As I was sourcing images for the book, I received generous assistance from Dr Máire Kennedy, Special Collections Librarian, Dublin City Library, whose willingness to help made my task much less daunting. My thanks also to Sandra McDermott, of the National Library of Ireland, Louise Morgan of the National Gallery of Ireland, Dr Charles Benson and the librarians of Early Printed Books Department of Trinity College Library. Reg Johnson has kindly allowed me to use balloon illustrations from the papers of Robert Tressell, the Dublin-born author of *The Ragged Trousered Philantropists* (1914). Images provided courtesy of the board of Trinity College are from J.E. Hodgson's *The History of Aeronautics in Great Britain*. Princeton University Press and the Public Record Office of Northern Ireland have also allowed the use of images.

I am very grateful to Anne O'Connor for her careful proofreading and for her advice throughout, and to Julia Barrett who also provided

Bryan MacMahon.

valuable assistance. Terry Connaughton, Artistic Director of Ranelagh Arts Festival has been a very enthusiastic supporter and is passionate in promoting awareness of Crosbie's achievements in Ranelagh and further afield. I am grateful to Brian White of Bray Cualann Historical Society for information on the Crosbie burials in St Paul's, Bray. In order to compare Crosbie's expenses with today's values, I have used the currency converter on the website of the British National Archives. I am grateful to Clive O'Connor for alerting me to the website www.measuringworth.com where estimates are almost double those I have used here.

A special word of thanks to Frank McNally of *The Irish Times* who, with encouragement from Terry Connaughton, has taken a keen interest in the story of Richard Crosbie. In a book which relies so much on newspaper accounts for details of Crosbie's exploits, it is fitting that a journalist should write the foreword. I am also grateful to Tom McCormack, artist and doyen of Irish ballooning, and current president of the National Aero Club of Ireland. My first experience of the thrill of balloon flight was courtesy of Tom.

Dr Linde Lunney of the *Dictionary of Irish Biography* project of The Royal Irish Academy, who has a special interest in the career of James Dinwiddie, has very generously spent time in reading the manuscript and I appreciate the many suggestions she offered for improvements.

Any errors or omissions are my own responsibility.

Finally, I wish to thank my wife Catherine for her support and patience while this work was being completed, and for her enthusiasm for the project. I grew up in Ballyheigue, where the Crosbies had been landlords for over 200 years, and I first read about Richard Crosbie in the 1960s in a parish history by Joseph Moriarty called *Ballyheigue Beside the Sea*. I had a long-term plan to research his life sometime, but the realisation that 2010 marked the 225th anniversary of his flights meant that the research and writing took on an unexpected urgency.

SOURCES

Research for this book began with a seminal article by F.E. Dixon entitled 'Ballooning in Dublin' in *Dublin Historical Record*, 1955. Fred Dixon was a professional meteorologist with a passionate interest in the history of his adopted city of Dublin. Without his article, it would have been very difficult for me to get started. I have returned to Dixon's article many times and have been constantly amazed at how much detailed information it contains, in a succinct style. I believe the article has been the unacknowledged source of many newspaper articles on ballooning. The Dixon Collection of slides held in Dublin City Library and Archive also contains several of the images used in this book.

The research done by Tom Cranitch has also helped me greatly. Tom was one of the first to champion Crosbie's cause, at the time of the bicentenary of his achievements in 1985. When a small harbour air-port was proposed for the Clontarf area in 1988, Tom suggested that it be named after Richard Crosbie. Liam Byrne has also written about Crosbie, and I obtained valuable information in his book. Likewise, Larry Walsh's article in the *Old Limerick Journal* gives a very detailed account of Crosbie's Limerick adventure.

More recently, two academic articles, one by Dr Linde Lunney and the other by Dr Barbara Traxler Brown, focus on specific aspects of Crosbie's career, and they were also a great help in providing specialist information and specific references on which I could build my research.

For an understanding of how Crosbie fitted in to the story of European ballooning, I am deeply indebted to the work of L.T.C. Rolt and J.E. Hodgson, and a more recent book by Richard Holmes. I have relied on these books for a broader understanding of the great ballooning adventures of the late eighteenth century.

I have benefitted greatly from on-line research for the new information included here in Chapter 10. The discoveries about Crosbie's hidden life in America came through the medium of various search-engines. Having acquired the references, I was surprised and gratified to find that information was readily available from archives in America, England and France.

BIBLIOGRAPHY

'A Masonic Incident in the Early History of Baltimore,' in *Masonic Review*,Vol. 66, No.6 (January 1887). Cincinnati, Ohio. pp 321–328. Hathi Trust Digital Library, www.hathitrust.org.

An Accurate and Impartial Account of the Apprehension, Trial and Execution on the 5th of June 1798 of Sir Edward William Crosbie, Bart. Published in justice to his memory by his family. (Bath, printed by R. Cruttwell. Dublin, reprinted by William Porter, 1802).

Aeronautica, or Voyages in the Air (1823).

Auster, Paul, *The Red Notebook* (New Directions: New York, 1995).

Barrington, Johah, *Personal Sketches of His Own Times* 3 Vols (Kessinger Publishing: London, 1830–32).

Boydell, Brian, *Rotunda Music in Eighteenth-Century Dublin* (Irish Academic Press: Dublin, 1992).

Boyd, Gary, *Dublin 1745-1922: Hospitals, Spectacle and Vice* (Four Courts Press: Dublin, 2006).

Burke's *Irish Family Records* (1976).

Burke, *General and Heraldic History of the Commoners of Great Britain and Ireland* (1838).

Butler, Richard, *Some Notices of the Castle and of the Ecclesiastical Buildings of Trim* (1854). Re-published by Meath Archaeological and Historical Society (1978).

Byrne, Liam, *A History of Aviation in Ireland* (Blackwater Press: Dublin, 1980).

Cavallo, Tiberius, *The History and Practice of Aerostation* (London, 1785).

Craig, Maurice, *Dublin 1660-1860: The Shaping of a City* (Liberties Press: Dublin, 1952). Re-published 2006.

Cranitch, Tom, 'The Beginning: The Balloon Era', in Liam Skinner and Tom Cranitch, *Ireland and World Aviation: The Complete Story* (Universities Press: Dublin, 1988).

Dickson, David (ed.), *The Gorgeous Mask: Dublin 1700-1850* (Trinity History Workshop: Dublin, 1987).

Dixon, F.E., 'Ballooning in Dublin', *Dublin Historical Record* Vol. XIV, No. 1 (June 1955).

Dunlap, William, *A History of the American Theatre* (London, 1833). On-line resource.

Dunlap, William, *Diary of William Dunlap 1766-1839: The memoirs of a dramatist, theatrical manager, painter, critic, novelist and historian* (New York, 1930).

Edgeworth, Frances A. B., *A Memoir of Maria Edgeworth, with a selection from her letters* Vol 1 (London, 1867).

Fagan, Patrick, *The Second City: Portrait of Dublin, 1700-1760* (Branar: Dublin 1986).

Farrell, William, *Carlow in '98.* (1949). Re-published as *Voice of Rebellion: Carlow in 1798. The Autobiography of William Farrell*, ed. Roger McHugh (Dublin, 1998).

Ferrar, John, *History of Limerick* (1787).

Gibbs-Smith, Charles H., *Ballooning* (Penguin Books: London 1948).

Gilbert, J.T., *A History of the City of Dublin* 3 Vols (Dublin, 1854–1859).

Gillispie, Charles Coulton, *The Montgolfier Brothers and the Invention of Aviation 1783-1784* (New Jersey, 1983).

Hodgson, J.E., *The History of Aeronautics in Great Britain* (Oxford University Press: Oxford, 1924).

Holmes, Richard, *The Age of Wonder* (Harper Press: London, 2008).

Hopkins, Frank, *Hidden Dublin: Deadbeats, Dossers and Decent skins* (Mercier Press: Cork, 2007).

Hopkins, Frank, *Rare Old Dublin: Heroes, Hawkers and Hoors* (Marino Books: Cork, 2002).

Ireland, Joseph Norton, *Records of the New York Stage from 1750 to 1860* (New York, 1867). Online resource.

Keen, Paul, 'The Balloonomania: Science and Spectacle in 1780s England,' *Eighteenth Century Studies*, Vol. 39, No. 4 (Summer 2006).

Kelly, Deirdre, *Four Roads to Dublin: a History of Ranelagh, Rathmines and Leeson Street* (O'Brien Press: Dublin, 1995).

Kelly, James, *That Damn'd Thing Called Honour: Duelling in Ireland 1570-1860* (Cork University Press: Cork, 1995).

Kelly, James, *The Liberty and Ormond Boys: factional riot in eighteenth century Dublin* (Four Courts Press: Dublin, 2005).

Leeson, Margaret, *The Memoirs of Mrs. Leeson, Madam, 1727-1797* ed. Mary Lyons (The Lilliput Press: Dublin, 1995).

Linehan, Maurice, *Limerick: Its History and Antiquities* (1866).

Longford, Elizabeth, *Wellington: The Years of the Sword* (Smithmark Publishing: New York: 1989).

Lunney, Linde, 'The Celebrated Mr. Dinwiddie: An eighteenth century scientist in Ireland', *Eighteenth Century Ireland – Iris an Dá Chultúr*, Vol. 3, 1988, pp 69-83.

Manuscript of Ambrosia Lifford letter. PA 1464. (Coventry Heritage and Arts Trust Library.)

MacMahon, Bryan, *The Story of Ballyheigue* (Baile Ui Thaidhg, 1994).

Manuscripts and Correspondence of James, First Earl of Charlemont, Vol II (1784-1799.) Historical Manuscripts Commission, Thirteenth Report, Appendix, part VIII (London, 1894).

Marion, Fulgence, *Wonderful Balloon Ascents* (London, 1870).

Maxwell, Constantia, *Dublin under the Georges 1714-1830* (Faber and Faber: London, 1956).

BIBLIOGRAPHY

McGuire, James & Quinn, James, (eds) *Dictionary of Irish Biography from Earliest Times to 2002* (Cambridge University Press: Cambridge, 2009).

O'Connor, Tommy, *Ardfert in Times Past* (Foilseacháin Bréanainn: Ardfert, 1999).

O'Keeffe, John, *Recollections of the Life of John O'Keeffe* (1826).

O'Brien, Gillian & O'Kane, Finola, *Georgian Dublin* (Four Courts Press: Dublin, 2008).

Rolt, L.T.C., *The Aeronauts* (1966). Re-published as *The Balloonists* (The History Press: Stroud, 2006).

Revue Brittanique, (1834). (Saulnier fils et P. Dondey-Dupré). On-line resource.

Potain, Dr, *Relation Aérostatique dédiée a la Nation Irlandaise* (Paris, 1824).

Plunket, Peg, *The Life of Mrs. Margaret Leeson alias Peg Plunket, written by herself*, 3 Vols (Dublin, 1798).

Sadler, James, *Balloon: An Authentic Narrative of the Aerial Voyage of Mr. Sadler across the Irish Channel* (Dublin, 1812).

Sadler, Windham, *Aerostation; A Narrative of the Aerial Voyage of Mr. Windham Sadler across the Irish Channel* (Dublin, 1817).

Stephens, Patrick, with Lausanne, Edita, *The Romance of Ballooning: The story of the early aeronauts* (The Viking Press: New York, 1971).

Tissandier, Gaston, *Histoire des Ballons et Aeronauts Célèbres 1783-1790*, 2 Vols, (Paris, 1890).

Traxler Brown, Barbara, 'French Scientific Innovation in late-Eighteenth Century Dublin: the Hydrogen Experiments of Richard Crosbie (1783-1785)' in *Ireland and the French Enlightenment, 1700-1800*, eds Graham Gargett, Geraldine Sheridan (London, 1999).

Watson's Almanack and Directory, 1786.

Walsh, J.E., *Sketches of Ireland Sixty Years Ago* (London, 1847).

Walsh, Larry, 'Richard Crosbie's Aerial Voyage from Limerick, 1786' in *Old Limerick Journal* (No. 31, Winter, 1994).

Whyte, Samuel, 'To Richard Crosbie Esq., on his attempting a Second Aerial Excursion in which he proved unsuccessful' (Grafton Street, Dublin, May 1785).

Whyte, Samuel, *Poems on Various Subjects,* (Dublin 1795).

Wemyss, Francis Courtney, *Chronology of the American Stage from 1752 to 1852* (New York, 1852). On-line resource.

NEWSPAPERS AND MAGAZINES CONSULTED:

Volunteer Journal
Dublin Evening Post
Faulkner's Dublin Journal
Freeman's Journal
Limerick Chronicle
The Times
The Irish Times
Walker's *Hibernian Magazine*
The Gentleman's Magazine

INDEX